DAY WALKS OF THE
West Coast
SOUTH ISLAND

DAY WALKS OF THE
West Coast
SOUTH ISLAND

MARK PICKERING

REED

FRONT COVER: Take the Harihari Coastal Walkway (38) along a splendid beach to the headland.
BACK COVER: Kahikatea forest grows at the edge of Ara o Te Iringa — Iveagh Bay (28).

Reed Publishing **(NZ) Ltd**
Te Karuhi tā tāpui o Reed (Aotearoa)

Established in 1907, Reed is New Zealand's largest
book publisher, with over 300 titles in print.

For details on all these books visit our website:
www.reed.co.nz

Published by Reed Books, a division of Reed Publishing (NZ) Ltd, 39 Rawene Rd, Birkenhead, Auckland. Associated companies, branches and representatives throughout the world.

© 2004 Mark Pickering
The author asserts his moral rights in this work.

ISBN 0 7900 0975 7

National Library of New Zealand Cataloguing-in-Publication Data
Pickering, Mark, 1953-
Day walks of the West Coast, South Island / Mark Pickering.
(Reed outdoors)
Includes bibliographical references.
ISBN 0-7900-0975-7
1. Hiking—New Zealand—West Coast—Guidebooks. 2. West
Coast (N.Z.)—Guidebooks. I. Title. II. Series.
796.51099371—dc 22

Maps by Chris O'Brien

Printed in New Zealand

Contents

List of Maps   8

Preface   9

Introduction   10
Landscape   10
Climate   12
Forest and wildlife   13
Maori history   14
  Pounamu   16
European history and the 1865 gold rush   17
Walking   20
  Safety   20
  Track grades   20
  New Zealand Environmental Care Code   21

Karamea and Granity Coast   23
  1 Heaphy Track to Scotts Beach   23
  2 Oparara Archways: short walks   26
  3 Fenian Valley and Cavern Creek Caves   28
  4 Chasm Creek Walkway   29
  5 Charming Creek Walkway   29
  6 Britannia Track   30
  7 Dennistoun Walkway   31
  8 Lyell Walk   33

Paparoa Coast   35
  9 Cape Foulwind Walkway   35
  10 Charleston: short walks   36
  11 Fox River and Fox River Cave   37
  12 Trumans Track   39
  13 Bullock Creek and Cave Creek   40
  14 Pororari Gorge Track   42
  15 Punakaiki — Pancake Rocks   43
  16 Point Elizabeth   44

Reefton and Grey River/Mawheranui Valley   47
17 Kirwan's Hill   47
18 Murrays Creek Goldfield Circuit   48
19 Murrays Creek Goldfield: Lankeys Creek   49
20 Alborns Coalmine   50
21 Waiuta: short walks   52
22 Snowy Battery and Powerhouse Circuit   53
23 Nelson Creek: short walks   55
24 Croesus Track: Garden Gully Stamping Battery   57
25 Croesus Track: Ces Clarke Hut and Croesus Knob   58
26 Arnold River Power Station Walk   59

Lake Brunner   61
27 Rakaitane Walk — Moana   61
28 Ara o Te Iringa — Iveagh Bay   62
29 Bains Bay — Mitchells   63
30 Carew's Creek Waterfall — Mitchells   63

Hokitika and Lake Kaniere   65
31 Kumara — Londonderry Rock   65
32 Goldsborough Track and Roadside Tunnels Track   67
33 Kaniere Water Race   68
34 Kahikatea Forest Walk   70
35 Lake Kaniere Walkway   71
36 Hokitika Gorge   73
37 Ross Goldfields Water Race Walk   73

Lagoons and Glaciers   77
38 Harihari Coastal Walkway   77
39 Okarito Pack Track   79
40 Franz Josef Glacier/Ka Roimata o Hine Walk   81
41 Franz Josef Glacier/Ka Roimata o Hine:
   short walks   83
42 Franz Josef Glacier/Ka Roimata o Hine:
   Lake Wombat and Alex Knob   84
43 Franz Josef Glacier/Ka Roimata o Hine:
   Point Roberts Track   85
44 Fox Glacier/Te Moeka o Tuawe Walk   86
45 Fox Glacier/Te Moeka o Tuwae: short walks   87
46 Lake Matheson   88
47 Gillespies Beach and seal colony   89

South Westland and Haast   93

  48 Paringa Cattle Track   93
  49 Monro Beach   95
  50 Ship Creek — Dune Walk and Swamp Walk   96
  51 Hapuka Estuary   97
  52 Jackson Bay/Okahu — Smoothwater Bay   99

List of Maps

Karamea and Granity Coast   22
Paparoa Coast   34
Reefton and Grey River/Mawheranui Valley   46
Lake Brunner   60
Hokitika and Lake Kaniere   64
Lagoons and Glaciers   76
South Westland and Haast   92

Preface

The West Coast of the South Island — or as the locals call it, 'The Coast' — is a vast area, stretching from the Heaphy Track in Kahurangi National Park to the north, down to Jackson Bay/Okahu in the south. The range of walks found here is astonishing. This is the first guidebook covering day walks of the West Coast, and is intended for both the Kiwi and overseas holiday-maker, or locals who are interested in exploring their own backyard.

Approximate travelling times and a track grade are provided for each walk, though times will vary according to weather and the fitness of your party. There is also information on easily accessing each walk as well as a brief description and detailed track notes. Points of interest are added to highlight the historical, wildlife and landscape features of each area.

Many well-known tracks have not been included, because they were more suited to tramping trips than walking, for example around Rahu Saddle (just outside of Springs Junction), and the areas inland from Hokitika such as the Whitcombe, Toaroha, Kokatahi and Styx rivers. My book *101 Great Tramps in New Zealand* has detailed information on these and other areas.

Over the years I have been asked by some mothers to provide a book of family walks; this isn't it, but I have indicated those walks that are suitable for younger children. Some of these walks have been tested by a five year old!

A compact guidebook such as this cannot completely cover the wealth of walking opportunities found in the West Coast, but it has included the best of them.

Mark Pickering

Introduction

Landscape

The West Coast of the South Island has always been different, and much of this difference can be attributed to its climate and its landscape. The Southern Alps/Ka Tiritiri o te Moana are basically on the West Coast's back doorstep, rarely more than 20 km from the shoreline. These mountains maintain a constant benevolent and brooding presence over the whole region.

Steep mountain rivers run down through granite gorges and cut across the coastal strip. In times of flood these rivers can wash out many single-lane bridges on State Highway (SH) 6, so sections of the province can become isolated very quickly. Few regions in New Zealand are as dependent on a single highway, and road maintenance gangs are a constant sight throughout the West Coast.

In many places thick, natural forest runs down to the highway and even to the shoreline, making this one of the few places in the country where a mountain-to-sea forest exists in its original state. Despite the relative absence of flat land there are a large number of lakes, some in almost pristine condition, and many with fine kahikatea or rimu groves along their edges.

The constant battering from westerly winds brings huge precipitation to the West Coast, as well as high snowfall to the icefields which have enabled glaciers such as the Fox and Franz to penetrate through the rainforest down to near sea level.

As a reminder of the West Coast's turbulent geological past there are 20 or more hot springs scattered throughout the mountains and rivers, and the great geological faultline, the Alpine Fault, has separated the West Coast granites from the Canterbury greywacke and Otago schists. Some West Coast rivers, such as the Taramakau and Landsborough, owe their unusual straightness to the fact that they follow the Alpine Fault.

The West Coast has a huge shoreline, wild beaches piled high with driftwood brought down by the great rivers. Early explorers recall needing to set fire to the driftwood, just to make a space to put up their tents. There is only one natural harbour along the whole shoreline at Jackson Bay/Okahu, and both Grey River/Mawheranui and the Buller are dredged to maintain them as useable, if dangerous, harbours. Every year some fishing boats and fishermen get lost on these notorious bars.

In all, the West Coast has a tough, turbulent landscape, and is one of the last and largest areas of New Zealand that still has a wilderness that existed before the arrival of Maori.

A low to mid-tide is essential for walking the beach section of Okarito Lagoon (39).

Climate

The weather is itself a powerful presence on the West Coast, and every visitor suspects it must affect the character of the people, the West Coasters, who live there. Visitors frown at the tatty farmland and the decrepit fence posts smothered in profusions of moss and lichen. 'Does the broodiness of the clouds encourage introspection and depression? Does the rainfall drive you to madness?' West Coasters develop standard responses: asked by a visitor if the rain would ever stop the West Coaster laconically replies, 'Well, it usually does.' And while it is unlikely there are more madmen on the West Coast than anywhere else, there are plenty of bush philosophers, and that might have something to do with the long days of rainfall.

The weather statistics are surprising: Hokitika, on average, gets about the same sunshine hours as Christchurch, though the rainfall is approximately 3000 mm a year compared to Christchurch's 800 mm; Hokitika receives about 180 rainy days, compared to Christchurch's 100 days of rainfall; any area of flat land on the coast this is away from the mountains usually gets better weather, especially during the drier months of winter; rainfall in Haast during August can be less than 100 mm, which is more surprising considering the annual average, like Hokitika's, is approximately 3000 mm.

For the record books, the aptly named Waterfall Rain Gauge situated in the Cropp River, which is a tributary of the Whitcombe River just inland from Hokitika, holds the New Zealand record for highest annual rainfall — 14.4 m in the 12 months to November, 1983 — enough rain to submerge a four-storey building. Milford Sound settlement, on the other hand, gets only a piddling 6 m of rainfall each year, although one rain gauge close to the Sound has recorded up to 13 m in a single year.

If these figures seem astounding, then there is one more rainfall record to literally drown you in disbelief. Alex Knob at Franz Josef Glacier/Ka Roimata o Hine is a low peak right on the edge of the mountains, at the height where breaking rainstorms are likely to be most intense. In March 1982, after a dramatic storm in the Franz Josef settlement, a park ranger made the arduous slog to the top of this low peak to record a rainfall of 181 cm in just three days.

Forest and wildlife

There are two predominant forest types on the West Coast: podocarps and beech forest. The former occupy mainly the beech forest 'gap' between the Buller and Paringa rivers, and is composed of the graceful rimu, tall kahikatea and the sturdy matai and miro. Within the mid-level podocarp forest, rata dominates, and flowers magnificently at Christmas time. The Australian brush-tailed possum — an introduced mammal brought in to establish a fur trade — particularly likes rata foliage and this has led to a considerable loss of rata on the coast.

North and South Westland are predominantly beech forest, with red beech on the lowland areas and silver or mountain beech higher up. At the sub-alpine level, there are dracophyllums such as the twisted mountain neinei (or pineapple tree, a reference to its lookalike leaves), turpentine scrub and olearias.

In the tussock and herbfields at the true alpine level there are numerous flowering plants, including gentians and celmisias. All now flourish with the reduction of red deer populations, thanks to the helicopter-culls of the 1970s and 80s. Other introduced animals found here include goats (such as chamois and thar), pigs, stoats, weasels, ferrets and wild cats.

Weka are just one of several native bird species found on the West Coast.

13

Consequently, native bird populations particularly the kiwi struggle under the onslaught of so many introduced predators. The kiwi population is managed intensively by the Department of Conservation (DoC) in places such as Okarito. Even so, taking any walk in the forest you should see and hear good numbers of fantail or piwakawaka, bellbird or korimako, grey warbler or riroriro, wood pigeon or kereru and brown creepers. Bush-clad lakes are a good place to both hear and see kaka, and the inquisitive kea are visible in popular tourist carparks, particularly at the glaciers. Weka are in abundance around Cape Foulwind, and it should be possible to at least hear a kiwi at night if you are camped in bush areas in South Westland.

Maori history

Maori first reached the West Coast in approximately AD 1200–1300, though what brought them here is a matter of speculation; curiosity, a search for new land to settle or population pressures may have all been factors. It is likely that Maori kept to the coastline when they first arrived, scouting for food sources, and travelling would have been easier along the sea beaches.

Greenstone, or pounamu, was probably first noticed on West Coast beaches before the source was traced inland to such rivers as the Arahura, so it is possible that this process of exploration led Maori to the central divides. By the time Europeans arrived, Maori knew all the main passes — so for the European, exploration of the West Coast was a rediscovery of a landscape already widely known.

Early Maori routes followed the easiest pathways, and in the South Island this usually means a valley rather than a ridge trail. There is evidence of some trail constructions such as ladders (the Miko Cliffs a famous example), manuka brush in swamps, and narrow chasms that might be bridged by poles or vine suspension bridges. Deep rivers were crossed by either swimming or by rafts or mokihi, which were made out of flax or harakeke stalks.

Clothing was basic; an all-purpose rain cloak, or pake, that left the legs free, and strong flax sandals or paraerae. Maori would carry several pairs of paraerae, repairing or making more as needed while travelling. Thomas Brunner, noted European explorer of New Zealand during the mid 1800s, wrote that these sandals took 20 minutes to make and lasted two days' hard travel. Special leggings, warmer 'undercloaks', and sandals were all

Flax or harakeke is a hardy plant seen throughout the South Island's West Coast.

used for the harsher conditions of some alpine trails, and ropes would also be carried for these alpine routes.

Maori exploited the food sources of both land and sea of the West Coast. From the sea margins came several species of fish, eel or tuna, whitebait or inanga, shellfish or pipi, seaweed or rimurimu and sea anemone or humenga. On the land, hunting and preserving bush-birds such as weka, kaka and kereru was crucial, especially during the summer, for the winter months ahead. The Maori dog, or kuri, was trained to catch birds, and could itself become a meal if food was short. Native vegetables included mamaku, nikau palm kernel, taro and crops of kumara but potatoes, once introduced, quickly became a staple. Inanga, tuna or fern root were smoked or dried and carried in kete, bags made of kelp or flax, for leaner times when it was not possible to live off the land.

A 'fire plough' or fire kete was also carried and because of its importance entrusted to a senior woman or wahine of the party. Family groups travelled slowly, though war parties could make very fast time across land or sea.

Perhaps the most famous Maori journey of all was Te Puoho's war party of 40 warriors and women, who travelled from Golden Bay down the

15

length of the West Coast, over the Haast Pass/Tioripatea to Southland (some 1500 km) during 1836–37. It was an ambitious but foolhardy raid which ended in death for Te Puoho and enslavement of his party with one exception — Ngawhakawawa, Te Puoho's brother-in-law. He alone managed to slip away from the clutches of the Southland Maori and retrace the terrible journey back to Golden Bay. Ngawhakawawa's is one of the greatest solo treks recorded in the history of the West Coast.

Historically speaking, the population of Maori in Westland is difficult to estimate. In 1857, Chief Tarapuhi at Mawhera Pa told James Mackay there were 87 Maori on the coast, and by 1868 the crown census registered 116 Maori (68 in Westland, 48 in Buller).

Pounamu

The precious stone pounamu is also known as greenstone and nephrite, or in other countries as jade. Large natural deposits of pounamu can be found in the West Coast in the Arahura and Wakatipu regions, in many rivers and beaches between Jackson Bay/Okahu and Martins Bay, and in several places in Westland excavations have found pounamu manufacturing sites.

Maori recognise several types of pounmau: kahurangi or light-coloured, kawakawa or dark-coloured, inanga or milky-green (a particularly prized form, sharing the name for whitebait) and tangiwai or transparent, among others. Each different colour signalled different properties. Tangiwai is known also as bowenite, a related stone and a type of serpentine, and is called takiwai in the dialect of southern Maori. It has been found in most significant proportions at Anita Bay in Milford Sound/Piopiotahi; this particular area is also named Tauraka-o-Hupokeka, meaning 'the anchorage of Hupokeka', after Hupokeka, an early chief. Takiwai is a fine, clear pounamu and its name means 'tear water'.

The exceptional hardness of pounamu made it a highly desirable material for weapons of war, and its beauty meant it was fashioned into ornaments. One account refers to pounamu as kai kanohi or 'food for the eyes', and Chief Tuhuru, father of Tarapuhi, possessed a prized pounamu mere or short club of pounamu with this name.

More than anything else, it was the lure of pounamu that established the travelling routes across the divide. Only in the South Island could the valued mineral be found, with the most abundant sources in the Arahura and Taramakau valleys. Maori regularly travelled the trails of Haast Pass/ Tioripatea, Browning Pass/Noti Raureka, Harper Pass, Whitcombe Pass,

Lewis Pass and possibly Brodrick Pass — this knowledge accelerated the European exploration of these areas.

Pounamu is not always obvious in its natural state, as there is usually an outer layer of rock that could be any colour ranging from almost white to deep-brown. Maori traditionally looked for pounamu when it was wet — after storms or an outgoing tide when the stone was more easily distinguished. The best pounamu pieces were often found on the shoreline, having survived the natural grinding mechanisms of river and shingle.

European history and the 1865 gold rush

The West Coast was the first part of New Zealand to be charted by European explorers, yet for a long time it remained the most obscure. In 1642, Abel Tasman arrived by sea somewhere near the Paparoa Range and skirted the coast north. Turning the corner of Farewell Spit, Tasman had his famous contretemps with Maori in 'Mordenaers' Bay.

The next European arrival was Captain James Cook. His map of 1770 certainly looked like New Zealand; however, with no sheltered anchorage the West Coast received only a few brief notations: Mistaken Bay (now Big Bay), Cascades Point, Open Bay (now Jackson Bay/Okahu), Cape Foulwind and Cape Farewell. The first European expeditions were by Brunner and Heaphy in 1846, followed by Brunner alone in 1847–48, but what really put the West Coast on the map was the discovery of gold.

Leonard Harper reported gold at the mouth of the Taramakau as early as 1857, Rochfort noted some in 1859, and Lauper got colour from the Whitcombe River in 1863. Haast also noted some, and Maori were working some gold by the early 1860s.

Westland was isolated, no one was sure the gold was payable, and Otago had just struck it rich and was a far easier place to get to. But once the West Coast gold rush was on it came like fury. By the end of March 1865, the population of Westland (or West Canterbury as it was then known) had jumped to 5000 from a mere 200 the previous year. Figures record 2000 people in Hokitika at this time.

The peak of the gold rush did not last more than three years, from 1865–1868, and some towns enjoyed only a few months' existence before being forsaken. It was one long rush kept alive by rumour, a time when just the whisper of a find would send men, who were often working perfectly good claims, mining pell-mell in some fantastic and spurious goldfield.

In 1865 there were over a thousand gold prospectors working the marine terraces between Point Elizabeth (16) and Grey River/Mawheranui.

The vast majority of diggers earned little and spent it mostly on food and alcohol, and it was chiefly the storekeepers and the packers who really made any money. Working conditions were often miserable; rain, sandflies, mud, mosquitoes, rats, blowflies, dysentery, influenza and sudden death or injury was the reality. The romance of West Coast goldfields has been invented largely by later writers who never experienced it.

At the height of the gold rush the population came close to 30,000, with women constituting 10–12 percent of the total. Most diggers came from the British Isles, often via the Australian and American fields, but Irish, Italians, French, Germans, Poles, Americans, Greek, Swiss, Dutch, Scandinavian, Chinese, Spanish and Portuguese were all represented.

Many of the walks in this book owe their existence to the great goldrush, and follow goldminers' pack tracks or travel through goldminers' tunnels.

From Karamea down to Jackson Bay/Okahu, no region of the West Coast was exempt from the gold rush; prospectors fossicked from the black sands on wild beaches to the wilder headwaters of all of the major rivers of South Westland.

There was a culture and a language of gold: a 'duffer' was a dry claim; a 'duffers rush' was where no gold was found and the prospector who led it was likely to be in for a hard time; 'new chums' were the new arrivals on the goldfields; a 'hatter' was a digger who worked alone; 'surfacing' or 'beaching' was looking among the beach sands after stormy days to see if any gold had been thrown up; 'tucker ground' produced enough money for food only, a 'wages claim' comfortable, a 'riser' definitely a good ground (maybe even a rich ground), and a 'piler' or 'homeward bounder' the best of all — where a man could make his 'pile' and head home for Australia or England.

The reality was far from the dream. It has been calculated that the average digger would recover an ounce a week, about £2.12 shillings. Remembering that it was easy to spend £3 a week on food, especially in remote areas, these individual returns were not great.

There are many gold stories, and the best ones are actually true. In 1886 R.C. Reid — then a gold buyer for the Bank of New Zealand — was approached by three diggers. Reid found the £2000 he was carrying in notes still a few hundred pounds short to trade; the diggers, in just six weeks, had collected around 50 lbs of gold dust worth today over $300,000. Then there was the famous gold rush on a main street in Hokitika itself, and some obtained 40 ounces of gold for little work; this unexpected strike was traced eventually to a 230-ounce bag of Waimea gold that had been lost three months previously.

Between 1864 and 1867 the West Coast produced over one million ounces of gold, valued at over £5,000,000. It was a crazy, fascinating era, but it is not possible to follow every twist and turn of the great gold rush here. Hand-stacked tailings, rusting machinery, abandoned water races and old pack tracks are some of the more tangible reminders of this extraordinary period.

The West Coast has settled down since the mid 1860s. 'Black gold', or coal, has proved a more reliable resource than gold, and coal mining, timber milling (originally native but now exclusively exotics), dairy farming, sphagnum moss and tourism have become the major industries of the region. The population of the West Coast is currently close to 30,000 — roughly the same as at the height of the gold rush.

Walking

Safety

A few basic tips should keep everyone safe:

- check the weather forecast before going, and adjust plans accordingly.
- take adequate clothing, particularly for children. Caps, sunscreen, warm and waterproof jackets are ideal.
- water, some nibbles to eat and a hot thermos are useful.
- be fully prepared, as some walks may require topographical maps, a compass and full tramping equipment.
- all these tracks are well signposted and marked. Note that DoC marks it's tracks with orange triangles.
- do not hesitate to turn back if the weather turns foul, or people in your party are not feeling up to it.
- take a cellphone if you wish, but do not expect it to work everywhere on the West Coast.
- keep an eye on time, and do not start a major walk in the afternoon. You will be surprised how many search and rescue callouts are due to walkers being caught out by darkness.
- let someone know where you are going. Tell friends and family or use the visitor centre logbooks.

Track grades

Note that these grades are subjective and provided as a guide only. Tracks are graded according to length, gradient and surface.

1 EASY

Track surface is well marked, metalled and mostly flat, suitable for children. Approximately 30–40 minutes return.

2 MODERATE

Track will be clearly marked and well formed, but usually involves some short hill climbs. Approximately 1–2 hours return.

3 HALF-DAY

Track is well marked, may involve some stream crossings, and can be uneven with several short hill climbs. Approximately 3–4 hours return.

4 FIT AND FULL-DAY
Track is well marked, but may be steep with a big hill climb and go above the bushline. Approximately 5–7 hours return.

New Zealand Environmental Care Code

The saying 'Take only pictures, leave only footprints' is an essential part of everyone's walking gear these days. The natural environment can only be enjoyed if we look after it.

For some reason people do not seem to count lolly wrappers and paper tissues as litter, but please take your rubbish home with you. Be proactive, and remove other people's discarded rubbish.

Keep to the marked tracks to avoid making the trails too wide, thereby damaging plants.

Lighting fires should be avoided and fire bans strictly observed.

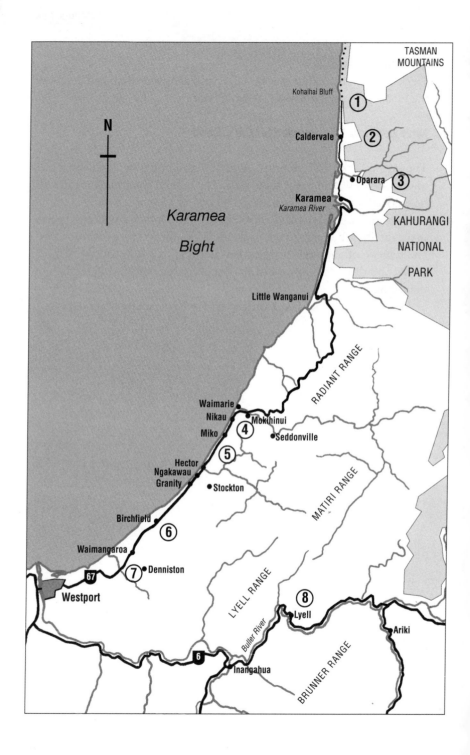

N

TASMAN
MOUNTAINS

Kohaihai Bluff
①

Caldervale ②

•Oparara ③

Karamea
Karamea River

Karamea

Bight

KAHURANGI

NATIONAL

PARK

Little Wanganui

RADIANT RANGE

Waimarie
Nikau •Mokihinui
Miko ④
•Seddonville

⑤

Hector
Ngakawau
Granity •Stockton

MATIRI RANGE

Birchfield

⑥

Waimangaroa

⑦ •Denniston

67

Westport

LYELL RANGE

⑧
•Lyell

•Ariki

Buller River

6

Inangahua

BRUNNER RANGE

Karamea and Granity Coast

Karamea is at the end of the road, an isolated and beautiful place that is worth the effort to reach, though relatively few people do so. Some of the best scenery on the West Coast is here including the magical Oparara Arches and the stunning seascape along Heaphy Track.

The Karamea Special Settlement of 1875–76 had a tough start, and the first 230 settlers were left largely to their own devices. Fortunately, these Shetland Islanders and English agricultural labourers proved adaptable and once they shifted from the pakihi or barren lands first given to them; the lowland pastures (once drained) proved good for stock, and Karamea remains a prime dairying area. There are plaques seen throughout the district commemorating the historic pioneering days.

Isolation was always a problem for Karamea, and it was not till 1915 that the first car got through The Bluffs. Now the road is excellent, if winding (I counted 170 bends!), and leads to this special part of the West Coast.

The Granity Coast runs from the Mokihinui River down to Westport, and here there are several superb short walks. Granity, Ngakawau and Waimangaroa are coal towns, and even today large amounts of coal are taken along the railway line to Greymouth and through the Otira tunnel to Christchurch. Almost every walk features some sort of mining history, whether it is to the remote gold battery of Britannia, or a climb up onto the misty, romantic tops of Dennistoun.

1 Heaphy Track to Scotts Beach

GRADE 2

TIME Scotts Beach two to three hours return. Nikau Walk 40 minutes return. Zig Zag Lookout Track 30 minutes return.

ACCESS From Karamea township it is a 15 km drive north to the Kohaihai River and road end. An extensive picnic and camping area is here, as well as toilets, shelter and telephone.

TRACK NOTES

Most children would handle the distance and hill, especially with the lure of the beach at the end. Unfortunately, the beach is not safe for swimming but there is plenty of sand and rocks and a sheltered picnic area.

The footbridge over Kohaihai River at the start of Heaphy Track (1) leads up the valley.

From the carpark, the track loops around the shelter, passes the Zig Zag Lookout Track and follows the Kohaihai River up the valley to the long swing bridge. Nikau Walk starts at the junction here.

The main track climbs steadily through nikau palms, karaka and rata, which can flower impressively during December. On the saddle there is a short track to a lookout towards Scotts Beach, then an easy descent to the sandy beach itself and a short distance further to the sheltered picnic area with toilets and drinking fountain.

POINTS OF INTEREST

The beach is wide and sandy with a rolling surf, and is safer for looking than swimming. The old Fisherman's Track to Scotts Beach, which provided an alternative route, is now overgrown and has been closed.

Maori used to cross the Gouland Downs on a route that is largely the same as today's Heaphy Track. James Mackay reached the Gouland Downs in 1857 from Aorere, and some diggers explored the route to Karamea by following down the Heaphy River a year later. The Heaphy was surveyed and cut as a track in the late 1860s, mainly as an access aid to gold-diggers, though it became overgrown. In 1893, a four-foot bridle track was established, but frequent slips soon made the route unserviceable. The Heaphy Track seemed to get only occasional usage until the New Zealand Forest Service built huts and upgraded the track in the 1960s. The creation of Kahurangi National Park in 1996 has made the Heaphy Track more popular and makes the likelihood of a road across this section rather remote.

Other good short walks from the picnic area include the Zig Zag Lookout Track (Grade 1), a steep ascent with several seats on the way overlooking the Kohaihai River, and the Nikau Walk (also Grade 1), a 40 minute loop through dense groves of nikau palms.

It is a step ascent to a great view from Zig Zag Lookout Track on the Heaphy Track (1).

2 Oparara Archways: short walks

GRADE 1

TIME Oparara Arch 40 minutes return. Moria Arch (or Little Arch) one hour return. Mirror Tarn 30 minutes return. Box Canyon and Crazy Paving Caves 20 minutes return.

ACCESS From Karamea township drive north for 10 km, then turn inland following the Oparara Archway signposts for 15 km to the carparks and

The pristine rainforest alongside the Oparara River is fun to explore and leads to both Moria and Oparara Archways (2).

walking tracks. The road is winding and narrow, though in reasonable condition.

TRACK NOTES

There are many short walks into pristine rainforest and alongside the photogenic Oparara River, an ideal choice for families, with many interesting things to see and do.

The track to the Oparara Arch starts from the carpark and information panel and follows a well-made track. After crossing a footbridge, the path turns and climbs inside the archway itself — dry and roomy with many stalactites and stalagmites — for a short distance.

Similarly, the track to Moria Arch (or Little Arch) starts from the same carpark, but is a little rougher than the Oparara Arch track and begins with a sharp climb. Then the track sidles around a bluff and drops to a river terrace, where walkers can amble through magnificent rainforest.

Walkers can clamber through a cave directly into Moria Arch itself, but signs warn against crossing the river. However, at low water take the upstream end onto a shingle riverbed for better views.

Other short walks in the Oparara area include the Mirror Tarn, where tall rimu and matai are reflected in a perfect pool, or up to the end of the road to the Crazy Paving and Box Canyon Caves. Both caves are easy and enjoyable for children to enter.

There is a mountain bike trail signposted halfway along the Oparara Archway access road.

POINTS OF INTEREST

The Oparara Arch is the largest natural structure in the Oparara basin, and may be the largest in New Zealand at 43 m tall and 219 m long. The Moria or Little Arch is smaller, at 19 m tall and 43 m wide.

Oparara is home to large bird populations, including great spotted kiwi, kaka, kea, tomtits or miromiro, bellbirds or korimako, parakeets or kakariki, wood pigeons or kereru, and tui. People frequently spot the rare blue duck or whio, coloured a grey and slate-blue with a white beak, on Oparara River. Males have a tell-tale whistling call or 'whio', and females a low, grunting call.

On the ground, look for the large-shelled powelliphanta snail, a nocturnal carnivore that feeds on worms. The shells are colourful spirals of brown, gold and orange. It is illegal to remove these creatures, or their empty shells. Rats, weka, and at times kea and kaka prey on these large snails, the largest of which may be 10–20 years old.

3 Fenian Valley and Cavern Creek Caves

GRADE 2–3

TIME Three to four hours return (including Caves Circuit Track).

ACCESS From Market Cross take the Fenian Road to the turn-off signposted 'Fenian Valley', then drive through the limestone quarry and continue to the carpark. Although the Fenian Track is alongside the Oparara River, it is not the access to Oparara Archways (2). Note: Do not park in the turning area itself because of falling rock.

TRACK NOTES

Although somewhat scrubby at first the road quickly becomes a first-class pack track as it follows the old goldminers' trail into the Fenian Basin. It sidles gently with occasional views of the river until reaching the distinctive rock overhang at Maloney's Bluff, a good place for a rest in the rain.

Shortly afterwards the track turns downhill and passes the first junction with the Caves Circuit Track, then through a deep man-made cutting and over the Cavern Creek bridge to the second junction with the circuit. Follow the main track to reach the unbridged Fenian Creek and carry on to Adams Flat (one hour).

It is best to start the Caves Circuit Track from the second junction, a circuit that would be enjoyed by older children (7–8 years and older). You will need a torch as well as scrambling skills, as one cave (the second of two) is unavoidable. The track is well marked with orange triangles and continues through confusing limestone country to reach Cavern Creek. Part of this creek goes partly underground, through caves and tunnels that can be explored with care at low flow, though you will at least get wet knees. The bottom surface is a thick sludge.

However, the main track continues past various entry and exit holes into Cavern Creek, before travelling in a complicated direction through a natural limestone 'cutting' at one point, then swinging down to the base of Tunnel Cave. You cannot avoid this short, 100 m cave, which climbs up a small creek, travels a zigzag around a waterfall, and climbs out. It is reasonably easy to negotiate and only at the little waterfall in the middle is it completely dark.

Follow the main track past the signposted Miner's Cave (entry and exit points the same) that winds back to rejoin the Fenian pack track.

POINTS OF INTEREST

The Fenian pack track was constructed in the late 1880s, and some gold digging continued here up to 1910. Chinese miners were reportedly working in this area. During the Depression, the government gave a 15 shillings-a-week subsidy to gold-diggers, though the Fenian was always considered a poor diggings. Many Irish nationalists, named 'Fenians', worked at gold digging on the West Coast.

4 Chasm Creek Walkway

GRADE 1

TIME 40 minutes return.

ACCESS On SH 67, just before the road climbs into The Bluffs section to Karamea, turn onto Seddonville Road and drive a kilometre to the carpark. The exit is only another kilometre down the road.

TRACK NOTES

This short walkway follows an old railway line through two deep cuttings to a tunnel that is 6 m high, and 80 m long. The tunnel is studded with glow-worms at night. Some good views of the Mohikinui River. Easy for children.

POINTS OF INTEREST

Mokihi means a raft of flax stalks and nui means large. In 1846, Charles Heaphy remarked, 'It was undoubtedly the most dangerous ford which I have met with in New Zealand.'

A gold town existed briefly at the mouth of the Mohikinui River in 1867, named Kynnersley after the then-resident commissioner. The location is now called Waimarie. Because the gold from here came in such flattened, waterworn nuggets they were affectionately known as Mokihinui Spuds.

5 Charming Creek Walkway

GRADE 2

TIME Three to four hours for the complete walkway (ideally with transport to pick you up at the other end). Two to three hours return to Mangatini Falls through the gorge.

ACCESS From Westport, drive 35 km north to Ngakawau. The walkway is signposted just before the river, 200 m to the carpark.

TRACK NOTES

Many interesting natural and man-made features on this walk and the first section to Watsons Mill shelter will be popular for children, as it includes two tunnels and a swingbridge.

From The Bins terminus you quickly follow the slick, dark waters of the Ngakawau River through the S-bend of Irishmen's Tunnel (a mistake in alignment), and through another tunnel — which is in fact a natural rock arch. The granite gorge is at its narrowest here as the tramway crosses a long suspension bridge that has spectacular views of Mangatini Falls.

There is another 50 m-long tunnel, a boardwalked verandah, and then the confluence of Charming Creek and Ngakawau River. The river always carries a thin line of foam and creates elaborate swirls and patterns as it joins the Charming. Just around the next corner is Watsons Mill, which has a toilet and shelter. A short, casual trail beyond the bridge descends to the picnic rocks by the dark tea-stained river.

From here on the walkway changes character, and leaves the gorge and enters a chewed-over forest of mining debris, relics of the old steam-sawmill, a sulphur hole and the Papa Tunnel. If you continue right through, either arrange transport to pick you up or allow two hours return (10 km extra).

POINTS OF INTEREST

At the warmer, coastal end of the walkway typical plants are the karamu, kiekie vine and kawakawa, with nikau palm and northern rata on the hill slopes overlooking the gorge. In the cramped and often gloomy spaces of the gorge itself there are silver beech and the unique *Celmisia morganii* daisy, found only in the Ngakawau Gorge.

Glow-worms can be present in the tunnels and by the wet, dark banks of the railway cuttings. They are the transparent carnivorous larvae of a gnat, living in a small tube from which are hung sticky, silky threads which trap their prey — mainly midges that are attracted to the luminescence. This luminescence has been calculated at one nanowatt (a thousandth of a millionth of a watt).

6 Britannia Track

GRADE 3

TIME Three to four hours return.

ACCESS From Westport travel north 20 km on SH 67 to a signposted side-road (it is easy to miss, but reads 'Britannia Track'). From here it is 1 km to a sheltered carpark and picnic area.

TRACK NOTES

It is a steady climb to the battery and a good half-day outing. The path starts, unpromisingly, along an overgrown vehicle track that leads over grass and scrub cow-paddocks (and possibly electric fences) to the bush edge. Once here you can amble along an excellent pack-track which soon reaches a junction with the Short Cut Track.

Stay on the main pack track as it climbs steadily over a footbridge and to the other end of Short Cut Track beside a seat. Shortly afterwards there is a signpost reading 'Great Republic Mine', and a 20 second side-track leads to a tunnel. This is approximately halfway to the Britannia Mine.

The track climbs steadily, winding in and out of bush gullies to a signpost. Follow the steep side-track down as it zigzags to the impressive renovated stamping battery.

POINTS OF INTEREST

The Britannia Battery was worked intermittently over several periods, as was the way with most gold ventures: from 1897 to 1910, then from 1925 to 1929 when it was damaged by the Murchison earthquake, and finally operated in the Depression from 1932 to 1936. The Department of Conservation renovated the stamping battery in 2003–04. The new, treated timber looks odd supporting the 100-year-old metal, but no doubt it will blend in over time.

For fit people, the return down the Short Cut Track is an attractive option although it crosses Stoney Creek twice — with skill walkers could boulder-hop without getting wet feet. This track passes the remains of the Great Republic Mine, including old tailraces.

7 Dennistoun Walkway

GRADE 3

TIME Four to five hours return, or two hours downhill one way.

ACCESS From Westport it is 15 km north on SH 67 to Waimangaroa, then Conns Creek Road to the carpark. Continue along Conns Creek Road to reach the historic site at the actual base of the incline. For access to the top of the walk, follow the signposted Dennistoun road as it climbs the 700 m plateau, and down the side-road to the carpark and lookout over the top of the incline. One Mile Log carpark is on the Dennistoun road and offers a shorter walk to the top. If you can arrange transport to drop you off at the top of the incline, the walking time is halved.

TRACK NOTES

A fairly difficult — and very rewarding — uphill walk. The walk goes through regenerating forest at first and past an old brickworks site, climbing 2 km to One Mile Log. From here the forest of tall rimu and red beech gets more substantial. This bridle track was built in 1884 when the hazards of riding down the incline wagons became only too obvious — someone was killed.

After two-thirds of the climb there is a short side-track to Middle Brake, where you get an idea of the uncomfortable steepness of the incline. An old viaduct is below Middle Brake but it is unsafe to go on; the incline itself is generally too steep and unstable to walk on.

Back on the main track, the last part to the top zigzags up stone steps to the lonely and rusting machinery at the top of the incline.

Other walks in the Dennistoun area include one to Coalbrookdale Mine (Grade 1, one hour return), where there are plenty of remains including the fan house, wagons, tramway tunnel and bridges.

POINTS OF INTEREST

The Dennistoun incline was built in 1878–79 and operated until 1967. It was proudly considered New Zealand's biggest and best engineering project at the time. Water-operated brakes slowed the coal-laden wagons (in a descent that was 1 in 1.20 over the 548 m drop) and helped pull up the empty wagons.

Some 250 miners and their families lived and worked on this bleak plateau at one time, and ultimately 12 million tons of coal were taken from Dennistoun. In 1887, Dennistoun coal town had three hotels, four general stores, three butchers, three bakers, one post office, a school and a resident population of 500.

A well-known coalworkers' rhyme:

'Damn Dennistoun.
Damn the track.
Damn the way both there and back.
Damn the wind and damn the weather.
God damn Dennistoun altogether'.

8 Lyell Walk

GRADE 1–2

TIME One to two hours return.

ACCESS Lyell is in the Buller Gorge, signposted off SH 6 approximately halfway between Murchison and Inangahua Junction. A large carpark, picnic and a camping area, with toilets, shelter and information boards, can be found here.

TRACK NOTES

The old Lyell goldfield is an excellent place for families to explore, and the walk to the stamping battery and back should be within the walking range of most children.

From the carpark, follow the good track past the cemetery — romantic looking with its many lichen–crusted headstones. The track descends and an elegant bridge crosses Lyell Creek. Just downstream from here is a historic diversion tunnel, dug by hand by the gold-diggers to divert Lyell Creek itself and enabling gold to be taken from the exposed creek bed.

The track then climbs steeply. At the junction turn right as the pleasant track winds along Lyell Creek and reaches a platform overlooking the historic ten-stamp gold battery. Return to the junction, and continue down the old dray road. This old road was the main road to the remote goldfield communities of Gibbstown and Zalatown. It crosses some slips and descends to the highway, crosses the Lyell River over the culvert and zigzags back up to the carpark.

POINTS OF INTEREST

The Lyell goldfield started life in November 1862, with several Maori prospectors finding gold. In January 1863 a 30-ounce nugget was found; around this time there were a hundred men at the Lyell, a mix of European and Maori gold-diggers. Access to Lyell was by canoe up the Buller River through a deep gorge, and in good weather this took three days. By 1882, Lyell was a sizeable town with a recorded population of 1070.

It was the discovery of the quartz mine of the Alpine Company that established Lyell as a true gold town. Quartz gold-mining remained productive up to 1912. Perched by the moody Buller River, cloaked in fine mist and surrounded by barely explored mountains, Lyell maintained a well-deserved reputation as the most romantic goldfield on the West Coast.

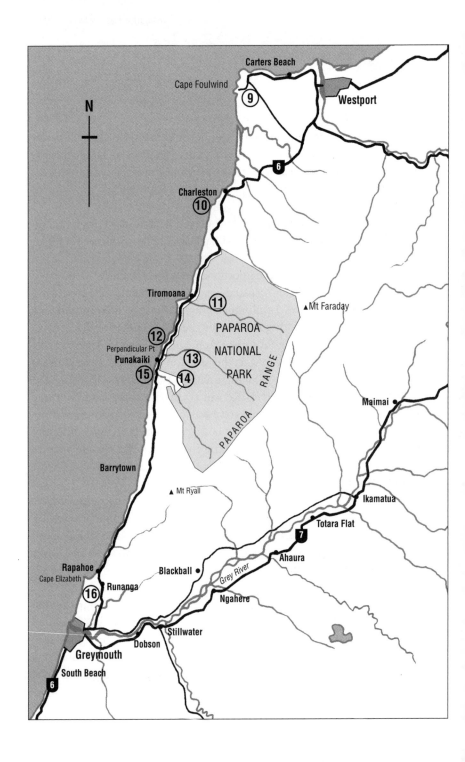

Paparoa Coast

The Paparoa coastline from Westport to Greymouth is one of the most dramatic in New Zealand. Parts of SH 6 are squeezed between the steep Paparoa mountain range and a foreshore of striking sea stacks, sandy coves, caves and sheer cliffs.

Most of these walks explore some aspect of the coast, from the seal colony at Cape Foulwind to the famous pancake rocks at Punakaiki. Here and there, walkers can find a few inland tracks and investigate the mysteries of the limestone syncline, or follow river canyons where rocks are perfectly reflected in the still green waters.

Punakaiki has become a busy community with new accommodation and shops springing up to cater for the visitors attracted to the famous blowholes and DoC's attractive visitor centre.

9 Cape Foulwind Walkway

GRADE 2

TIME 30 minutes return to the seal colony. One to two hours one way for the entire walkway.

ACCESS From Westport it is 12 km down the Carters Beach road to the large carpark and toilets at Tauranga Bay. A popular café is situated at the other end of bay. The northern carpark is beside the gorgeous Gibson Bay.

TRACK NOTES

This is a very popular walk that wanders along the dramatic headlands of Cape Foulwind. Children will enjoy the antics of the seals, and most should be able to complete the track one way.

From the carpark an excellent track climbs onto the headland and looks over the glorious golden sweep of Tauranga Bay. The track then leads past several lookouts over the seal colony.

At breeding time the colony is spectacular, with as many as 100 to 150 pups. The fur seal is found only in New Zealand waters and off the south coast of Australia, and the seals arrive to give birth in November and December. By March the numbers of pups are at their peak, and a lively lot they are.

From here the track is well graded and follows the cliff-tops with wonderful views. Beyond the lookout, the track sidles around to the lighthouse and onto the carpark — but just before here an unmarked trail leads down to the shore, and follows the banking of the old railway line that was used for moving quarried rock. On stormy days this is a wild piece of shore. Watch out for seals here, stragglers can often be spotted snoozing on the rocks.

POINTS OF INTEREST
Naming this cape has been a popular pastime for European navigators; in 1642 Abel Tasman named it 'Clyppygen Hoeck' or rocky corner; Cook called it 'Foulwind' in 1770; and in 1827 Dumont d'Urville called it 'Les Trois Clochers' or 'the three steeples'.

Cape Foulwind was the difficult part of the Charleston-Westport coach route of the 1860s, with a 'rough three miles' over the cape itself through heavy bush, before a short beach stretch again at Tauranga Bay and another cutting through the rocky peninsula onto Okari Beach. Several wayside houses sprang up to ease the traveller's thirst in what took a reasonable day's travel between the two towns.

The busy, flightless and inquisitive weka is often seen at the Cape Foulwind carpark. Its aggressive, curious nature has enabled the weka to cope with humans and their introduced predators. There are several sub-species of weka, including one found on the Chatham Islands. Weka eat a varied diet of berries, insects, lizards, mice, rats, young rabbits, shellfish, grasses, seeds, vegetable crops, snails and the eggs and young of other birds.

10 Charleston: short walks

GRADE 1
TIME 15 minutes (each walk).
ACCESS From SH 6 at Charleston, turn off at the signposted Constant and Joyce Bay road, and follow it to the extensive carpark and picnic area beside the bays. Both toilets and track entrances are found at the first bay.

TRACK NOTES
These two interconnected walks wander over flaxfields and around dramatic headlands on the coastline. It is an easy walk for children, but be cautious near the sea-cliffs.

The loop track follows a circle around one headland, then joins with the Lookout Track that climbs to a bare-rock viewpoint. Excellent views are had along the surf-crashing coast as far as Cape Foulwind.

The hooks drilled into the rock here are belay points for the rock climbers who abseil down to the tidal platforms and climb the short sea-cliffs.

POINTS OF INTEREST

In 1868, the raised sea beaches of Charleston were found to be rich in gold and the rush was on. Well over a hundred hotel names are recorded in Charleston from this period.

Another name for Charleston is Charlie's Town, so named after Captain Charles Bonner who was skipper of the ketch *Constant*.

The two tiny and pretty harbours — Constant Bay and Joyce Bay — have silted up considerably because of the goldfield tailings.

Gold digging at Charleston in the 1860s was a turbulent affair, as G.M. Hassing describes:

'All day on Sunday diggers flocked out to the new rush. My mates were three very decent, peaceful fellows, and we, in anticipation of the rowdyism that we knew would take place when pegging off would commence on Sunday night, deemed it prudent to look around for a fighting partner in case of emergency. We succeeded in picking up one, Pat Mullins, whose reputation as a bruiser of the first water was a house-hold word on the Coast. Indeed, it was well we provided for the onslaught, for the swearing and tearing and skull-cracking on that glorious Monday morning was really something to be remembered.'

11 Fox River and Fox River Cave

GRADE 2–3

TIME Two to three hours return to the cave.

ACCESS Off SH 6, roughly 10 km north from Punakaiki, cross the Fox River bridge and take the short signposted side-road to the carpark.

TRACK NOTES

Although this is a well-marked track there is some scrambling required at the end, particularly if you want to go into the cave. This walk will suit older children.

The marked track starts as a stopbank which merges into an old gold-diggers' pack track as it reaches the bush edge. This pleasant track crosses

The track to Fox River Cave (11) is on the north side of the river through the canyon.

two low bush spurs via old miners' cuttings. It crosses a dry side-branch of the Fox River, where the granite boulders glitter with quartz, and shortly afterwards reaches the first Fox River ford. Walkers heading up the Inland Pack Track cross the river here, but the track to Fox River cave remains on the north side of the river.

The route to the cave continues along a benched track, which gradually becomes rockier, and then follows a steep creek bed to the impressive cave entrance, which can be entered for a short distance. Take a torch.

POINTS OF INTEREST

During 1866–67, the gold boomtown of Brighton sprang up on the spit just north of Fox River. It is said that Brighton was the fastest growing gold town on the West Coast, rising from 50 business premises to 160 buildings and 53 hotels just two weeks later. Brighton's peak existence was for about four months when 6000 people were in residence.

Fox River was named after the prospector Bill Fox.

Te Oru Mata cave takes it's name from oru, a deep hole or cave, and mata, a headland. This spectacular T-shaped cavern was used by Heaphy, Brunner and Haast; the last found it comfortable if 'draughty'.

Access to the cave is via the old Fox River bridge, then following a track that goes underneath the modern bridge and past some baches to the cave entrance. At low tide it is possible to scramble through the cave and around the headland to the beaches.

12 Trumans Track

GRADE 2
TIME 40 minutes return.
ACCESS Travel 2 km north of Punakaiki to the signposted carpark.
TRACK NOTES
This is an easy, short and satisfying walk, with wonderful sea views and a rugged cove carved out of the rocks. Children will enjoy the sandy beach.

Shallow sea caves and coves carved out by the ocean are found along Trumans Track (12).

Follow the track through the coastal jungle of rimu, matai and entanglements of white-limbed kiekie and dark twisting supplejack. Then the track goes through a flax belt, and tough mats of coastal herbs, before reaching the upper sea-rock platform. Take care here as these rocks are notoriously greasy.

Steps go down onto the attractive and sandy semi-circlular beach, where shallow sea-caves have been carved out. The sea can rush in here with surprising force, so don't get caught out. At low tide it is possible to scramble around the sculptured rocks to the next bay and tidal platforms.

POINTS OF INTEREST

Flax or harakeke is a distinctive coastal plant, with stiff, red-petalled stalks that can grow up to 3 m tall. Nectar feeders such as tui, bellbird or korimako, and silvereye love the sweet juice and act as pollinators for the plant. Maori traditionally used this plant for many things including taura or rope, kete or baskets and paraerae or sandals. Flax leaves are used also for wrapping food in while it cooks.

13 Bullock Creek and Cave Creek

GRADE 2

TIME One to two hours return.

ACCESS From SH 6 about 2 km north of Punakaiki, drive up the narrow and winding Bullock Creek road. This road can flood after rain and is not recommended for caravans or campervans. It is an attractive valley with limestone bluffs leading to the carpark. Due to the flood danger, no overnight parking is permitted.

TRACK NOTES

This is an interesting walk into the heart of the Paparoa landscape on a well-graded and signposted track. The fascinating geology of the area is explained by good information signs. Families will enjoy this walk, although it is difficult scrambling on the river rock of Cave Creek itself.

From the Bullock Creek carpark it is a short stroll to the junction with the Inland Pack Track. Follow the signposts along the four-wheel-drive (4WD) track past the stone memorial.

The track then leaves the Inland Pack Track and twists down through the forest to Cave Creek and the staircase. Good information signs here display the complex relationship between Bullock Creek and Cave Creek.

Early morning mist over Bullock Creek (13).

If you travel downstream from the foot of the staircase and clamber over the slippery rocks, you will reach the resurgence where the creek gushes out from underground. Turning right from the staircase you will find a trail which leads past the cave entrance itself to a fence where a sign warns of the danger of falling rocks ahead; do not continue any further.

POINTS OF INTEREST

The Paparoa syncline is a complex limestone structure with bluffs, caves, overhangs, tomos (holes), gridges (chasms) and all manner of geological structures that are caused by water eroding the soft limestone. Bullock Creek has been 'captured' by the Pororari River, and flows underground to emerge as the Cave Creek resurgence. During heavy rain, parts of Bullock Creek flow into the Xanadu cave system, flooding it — sometimes this sudden influx of water has trapped cavers.

In April 1995, 14 young people on an outdoor education course were killed at Cave Creek when a platform they were standing on collapsed. This site therefore has great significance to the families of those killed. There is a memorial stone located at the start of the track, and walkers are asked not to go beyond the fence onto the accident site itself.

14 Pororari Gorge Walk

GRADE 2

TIME Two to three hours return from junction with Inland Pack Track.

ACCESS At Punakaiki itself, just 500 m north to a signposted carpark on the left-hand side.

TRACK NOTES

A pleasant, easy walk up the Pororari River, which suits a family outing, with gorgeous reflections in the river as you head upstream.

The track starts by ducking underneath the main road bridge then rambling along an easy trail with many splendid nikau palms. As the Pororari River narrows into its gorge, the track follows the river closely. There are many attractive rocks reflected in the still green waters.

At one point the track wriggles through a short cave, then follows the bush clad river's edge until you are through the gorge and in flatter bush. The Pororari River track meets the main Inland Pack Track at a signposted junction here. Travel north on the Inland Pack Track for 50 m to a beautiful ford in the Pororari River, which is a good spot to have lunch.

Examples of the attractive sculpted rocks found in the green waters of the Pororari River (14).

Some walkers prefer to take the right-hand track south along the Inland Pack Track, which crosses a low saddle and drops to the wide shingle of the Punakaiki River. There is a broad river crossing here, then follow the short road back to the main highway.

15 Punakaiki — Pancake Rocks

GRADE 1
TIME 30 minute circuit.
ACCESS The track starts opposite the Punakaiki information centre, café, tearooms, toilets, shop and large carpark.
TRACK NOTES
The Pancake Rocks are a peculiar rock formation with limestone layered in elegant towers. Surf surges into the caverns here, and with the right sea running can blast up through the blowholes underneath the rocks, creating a memorable short walk for everyone.

The track begins in coastal bush then dense flax or harakeke, and

The elegant towers of limestone at Pancake Rocks (15), and a view of the coast beyond.

circumnavigates a surging sea chamber. Good information signs are found at the many lookout points. These rocks were formed by shell debris sedimentation, which accumulated and compressed over millions of years before being uplifted.

Shrubs cling to the very edges of the blowholes, which have names like 'Sudden Sound', 'Chimney Pot' and 'Putai' or 'Seaspray'. On a clear day Aoraki/Mt Cook can be seen in the far distance, though often the Paparoa coast appears smoky from the heavy spray of the pluming sea.

POINTS OF INTEREST
The BBC television series *Walking with Dinosaurs* used the Pancake Rocks as a dramatic (and plausible) landscape background for their digitally created pterodactyls.

16 Point Elizabeth

GRADE 2
TIME Two hours to two hours 30 minutes one way.
ACCESS From Greymouth the south carpark is accessed via Cobden, then along the coast road for 4 km. The north carpark is found off a side-road from SH 6 just before Rapahoe (6 km from Greymouth).

TRACK NOTES
The track leaves the Rapahoe carpark and climbs to an old water race. This well-graded and gravelled track becomes a miner's road further on, and there is a brief view of the coast before the track reaches the Point Elizabeth headland at a junction.

Turn right and walk to the lookout platform that has good views of the islands. Back at the junction, continue ahead to the old miners' dam. The track sidles through dark groves of nikau palms along 'Darkies Terrace', an old gold mining area that was possibly named after 'Darkie' Addison, a well-known black prospector of the 1860s. The track gradually descends through scrub and flax to the shingle carpark beside the surging surf.

POINTS OF INTEREST
Much of this track was cut by the gold-diggers in 1865 to bypass the dangerous headland, and in December 1865 a thousand men were working the marine terraces between Grey River/Mawheranui and Point Elizabeth. Two suggested Maori names for Point Elizabeth are Matangitawau, matangi meaning breeze and tawau a mist or light smoke.

The track through nikau palm forest on Point Elizabeth Track (16) was originally cut by the gold diggers of 1865 so as to bypass the dangerous headland.

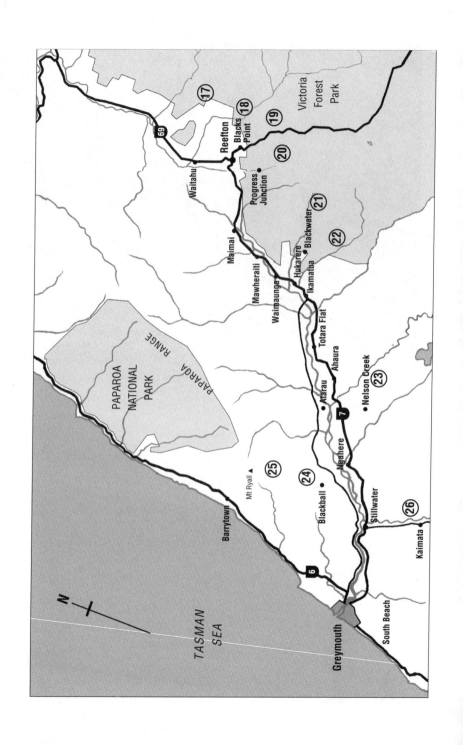

Reefton and Grey River/ Mawheranui Valley

Nearly all the walks in this section have been influenced by the great West Coast gold rush of 1865. It lasted only three short years, but in that time the landscape was stripped down to the gold-bearing gravels and covered with mine workings, shafts and old batteries. Many of the remains are still here, although many are smothered in the West Coast bush that has had the final say.

Kirwan's Hill (17) is a magnificent pack track to an alpine peak, while Murrays Creek Goldfield (18 and 19) has a network of trails following old miners' tracks. Both Big River and Waiuta (21) are romantically isolated, though Waiuta may not stay that way. The Croesus Track (24 and 25) is another historic pack track that crosses the range, and there is a side-trip to the well-preserved Garden Gully stamping battery. Nelson Creek (23) is riddled with old tunnels and tailraces that provide great fun for families to explore.

There is still gold in these hills and the Macraes Mining Company put forward a proposal is 2004 to extract it from Waiuta.

17 Kirwan's Hill

GRADE 3

TIME Eight to nine hours return (a full day).

ACCESS From Reefton, take SH 69 north for about 11 km and turn down Boatmans Road. Travel for 7 km to Capleston carpark. In 1877, this mining town boasted seven pubs for 1000 people; now there are just a few rusting car bodies decorating the paddocks.

TRACK NOTES

A brilliantly graded miners pack track leads up to a hut on a hill, where Aoraki/Mt Cook can be seen as well as a panorama of crinkled bush tops. It is a long day's tramp, but very rewarding.

From the carpark, a muddy vehicle track crosses farmland to the bush edge, and through a miners' tunnel for a short distance to a footbridge across Boatman's Creek. After this dramatic start the track ambles alongside the creek before crossing back and continuing to Topler Creek.

Once across Topler Creek (with no luxury of a footbridge) the pack track settles into a rhythmic zigzag for 8 km, climbing almost 900 m to Kirwan's Hill, and a short side-track to Kirwan's Hut. This hut has 12 bunks and a stunning view.

If you have the time, the 'Kirwan's Reward' open-cast mine site is worth a look. It is along the main pack track and down a short signposted side-track. There are views here of the 1898 aerial ropeway.

It is an easy romp down the pack track to Capleston — though your knees and thighs may be sore by the time you get back to the carpark.

POINTS OF INTEREST

Kirwan's Hill was named after the prospector William Kirwan, who in 1896 discovered a large area of gold-bearing quartz high on the hill that bears his name.

In 1898, the aerial ropeway was erected, linking the hillside quarry site with the stamping battery, some 550 m below. The ropeway was an impressive engineering structure and the Kirwan's Reward goldmine quickly proved profitable — in fact, the first investors doubled their money in 18 months. However, after 1907 most of the gold had been extracted and the mine changed hands several times as it became unprofitable and finally closed in 1909. Some prospecting went on during 1913–14, and the Depression of the 1930s.

18 Murrays Creek Goldfield Circuit

GRADE 2–3

TIME Four to five hours for Murrays Creek main track, returning via Royal Track (9 km return). The Royal Track is not well marked and can be overgrown, so would suit experienced walkers only. The goldminers' tracks on the Murray Creek and Royal Track circuit are generally well graded.

ACCESS Off SH 7 at Blacks Point, a kilometre from Reefton.

TRACK NOTES

The main Murrays Creek Track follows a broad pack track through luxuriant moss and beech forest, passing the junction to the Energetic Mine track (20 minutes return) and the bridges at Cement Town (ten minutes return). Not much remains, though gold was mined in Murrays Creek from 1870 until the 1930s.

Not long after this junction, the main track leads into a broad area of manuka forest at Chandlers Open Cast Coalmine, and reaches the Waitahu Track junction at a saddle. Keep to the main track as it climbs steadily to the Inglewood junction, and it is only a short side-track past the Painkiller Track junction to the iron remnants of the Inglewood Mine (40 minutes return to the site).

Take the Royal Track, which climbs up to another saddle and the remains of the horse whims: raised, circular embankments where horses walked round and round pulling coal carts.

Soon afterwards there is the Ajax Mine shaft (518 m deep) then the Ajax Battery, which is the most attractive of the gold ruins. The track is not so good from here, and climbs a mossy gully to another saddle. It is a long, steady descent almost 300 m on the way back to the main Murrays Creek track.

POINTS OF INTEREST
It was the alluvial strike by the Murray brothers in 1866 that gave the goldfield its name. Some early nuggets from the creek weighed up to 30 ounces.

Much of the gold was found in conglomerate rock known to the miners as 'cement' — hence Cement Town. Copper and even precious stones were found in this conglomerate though not in payable quantities.

Black Point Mining Museum is situated by the carpark.

19 Murrays Creek Goldfield: Lankeys Creek

GRADE 2–3
TIME One hour 30 minutes to two hours return.
ACCESS Lankeys Creek carpark is signposted off SH 7, 3 km east of the Black Point Museum and Murrays Creek carpark.

TRACK NOTES
Most walkers will do Lankeys Creek as a circuit from the highway carpark, though a historic pack track links Lankeys Creek with the Murrays Creek circuit tracks (18). This short circuit is a steep climb through attractive beech forest and then a tunnel, and would suit older children.

From the carpark, cross the farm paddocks and footbridge and slip into the beech forest. The track grade is gentle at first and then becomes steep as it passes metal remnants of the old gold mining industry.

Once up high the track sidles more easily, past the impressive entrance to the Bolitho Mine (along a side-track), before a short attractive tunnel and onto the junction with the Incline Track. This track zigzags down through beech forest and rejoins the main track by the creek.

POINTS OF INTEREST
The Tram Track (grade 2 to 3, two to three hours one way) between Lankeys and Murrays creeks is an interesting 6 km tramp with many historic mining features including collapsed tunnels, adits, sleepers and cuttings.

20 Alborns Coalmine

GRADE 2
TIME One hour to one hour 30 minutes for the circuit.
ACCESS Just south half a kilometre from Reefton off SH 7 is Soldiers Road. Drive about 9 km up this narrow and winding road to Alborn carpark.

TRACK NOTES
This short circuit embraces an area with several small coalmines, and a rich coal-mining history.

The brochure — available from the Reefton information centre and containing some interesting historical information — suggests that this circuit can be walked in 'shoes', but this should be taken with a pinch of salt as the track can get muddy in places.

From the carpark, stroll along the tramway to the track junction, then turn left and follow the track as it climbs through rolling manuka country, past several old mine sites and eventually winds around to the old coal skips. Shortly afterwards there is the side-track to Alborn Coalmine itself and the remains of a Leyland truck. The track then descends by the tramway back to the carpark.

POINTS OF INTEREST
The first coal extraction from this area was around 1880. The Alborn family took over the running of the old mine in 1923 and used various methods for shifting the coal to the railhead, including Chevrolet trucks and fluming. Coal was as essential as gold in the Reefton mining community for both running the steam engines and heating homes in the damp winters. The mine closed in the 1950s.

Big River is a well-preserved mining site, with poppet head tower and winding plant, cyanide tanks, pack tracks and old dam site, beech forest and DoC hut. It is some 12 km further along the Soldiers Road from Alborns coalmine carpark. Strictly for 4WD vehicles only, the road is not being maintained and fallen trees and snowfall can block the road and the fords can flood. Ordinary cars will not get beyond Alborns carpark. Allow a one way drive, one hour to one hour 30 minutes from Reefton.

A short side-track from Alborns Coalmine (20) leads to the remains of an old Leyland truck, used by the Alborn family in the 1920s.

21 Waiuta: short walks

GRADE 1

TIME 10 to 30 minutes.

ACCESS The Waiuta access road is 20 km south of Reefton on SH 7, just before Hukarere. This 15-km road is winding and narrow. An information sign and shelter is found at Waiuta on Top Road, and there are toilets opposite.

TRACK NOTES

Much of this area is appreciated better on foot and it is worthwhile parking the car at the information shelter and wandering around from here. There is a road circuit around Waiuta with many signs containing interesting historical information. It is a good area for families, though people should stick closely to the marked tracks.

The Swimming Pool walk (ten minutes) visits the old empty swimming pool and passes two prospecting tunnels. The Middle Track (20 minutes) begins from the information shelter and links Top Road with Bottom Road.

It is worth driving up Pro Road to the Prohibition Mine site. This road is rougher than the circuit road around Waiuta, but in reasonable condition for most vehicles. It passes the signposted track to Big River as it winds up

Debris from the heady days of gold mining can be explored in a walk at the Prohibition Mine site around Waiuta (21).

ABOVE: An early morning reflection in Bullock Creek (13), within the heart of Paparoa National Park.

ABOVE: Remains from one of New Zealand's biggest engineering projects of the early twentieth century — the Dennistoun incline — visible from the Dennistoun Walkway (7).

ABOVE: The West Coast has a dramatic shoreline that reflects the tough, turbulent landscape.

LEFT: Tidal platforms at Te Miko — literally, the young shoots of the nikau — just 3 km from Punakaiki.

BELOW: The powerful blowhole at Punakaiki — Pancake Rocks (15) makes for a memorable day walk.

ABOVE: One of several machine remnants of the gold rush days still visible at Croesus Knob on the Croesus Track (25).

ABOVE: A view of peaceful Lake Kaniere from the start of the Kahikatea Forest Walk (34).

ABOVE: Kea and rainbows at the Fox Glacier carpark.

ABOVE: Busy day at Lake Matheson (46), one of the most popular walking and photographing spots.

ABOVE: The aptly named Smoothwater Bay (52).

ABOVE: The sunset over Three Mile Beach, Okarito (39).

ABOVE: Lake Brunner at Iveagh Bay (28).

the Pro Road to the highest point of Waiuta. Old mining debris is strewn around, as well as very good information signs explaining the site. The Viewpoint Walk takes five minutes from the top carpark.

POINTS OF INTEREST

Waiuta began life with the discovery of the 'Birthday Reef' in 1905 by four gold prospectors on the birthday of King Edward VII. The prospectors sold it for £2000 to a speculator who subsequently sold it to the Consolidated Goldfields Company for £30,000.

The original mineshaft was named the Blackwater, but the mining company later switched to the Prohibition Mine on the hill. This became New Zealand's deepest mineshaft (879 m). The Blackwater shaft was still vital for ventilation and pumping for the many levels in the goldfield, so when this collapsed suddenly in 1951 it allowed poisonous gases into the Prohibition workings and Waiuta was abandoned. The mine had produced three-quarters of a million ounces of gold.

By the 1930s, Waiuta's population peaked at about 600 men, women and children, with over 100 pupils at the school. However, within three months of the mine's closure in 1951 only 20 families remained.

22 Snowy Battery and Powerhouse Circuit

GRADE 2–3

TIME Two to three hours return.

ACCESS The Waiuta access road is 20 km south of Reefton on SH 7, just before Hukarere. This 15-km road is winding and narrow. An information sign and shelter is found at Waiuta on Top Road, and there are toilets opposite.

The other access point to the Snowy Battery is 2 km before Ikamatua, turning onto the Hukarere or Snowy River road some 12 km to where signposts are visible on the other side of the river. There are no footbridges across the Hukarere; however, in normal flow it is relatively easy to wade across if you do not mind wet feet. In some ways this is the more attractive entry, even for families, as there is more to see here with both the powerhouse site and the Snowy Battery site readily accessible. The beech forest, with the gold-orange coloured river running through it, is particularly eye-catching.

TRACK NOTES

This walking circuit follows historic pack tracks and visits two significant mining sites. This description is written from the Waiuta access point as this does not involve any river crossings.

From the Snowy Battery signpost at Waiuta, walk down the rutted 4WD road to where the pack track starts and the Snowy Battery side-track signpost. The best route is the easy pack track as it winds gently down through manuka and beech forest to a junction near the Hukarere River.

Take the track down to the Powerhouse, where a chimney and some foundations remain. The powerhouse was driven by water from a water race and provided electricity for the township of Waiuta. Return to the junction and follow the track alongside the water race.

Do not drink any of the water found in the vicinity of historic Snowy Battery (22) — the original cyanide tanks and surrounding ruins can otherwise be safely explored.

Views of the Hukarere River, as the track climbs gradually to the Snowy Battery site, are particularly attractive. This dramatic mine ruin still has many of the original cyanide tanks and the 'Slime' silos standing. Note: Do not to drink water in the vicinity.

The return track steeply climbs many steps above the battery site before following a broad pack track. At one point this track intersects another pack track which can be followed a short distance to the mine site. However, the main track climbs through the forest and quickly reaches Waiuta again.

POINTS OF INTEREST

Rock containing gold quartz from the Blackwater was taken out by horse-pulled wagons and sent down the incline to Snowy Battery — a massive gold-extraction plant. The rock was pounded by a stamping battery and then washed over mercury to catch the fine gold. Other techniques involved large vats of cyanide that gleaned gold missed in the first stamping process.

23 Nelson Creek: short walks

GRADE 2

TIME One hour 30 minutes to two hours for the full circuit (Tailrace Walk, Tunnel Walk and Colls Dam Walk).

ACCESS Off SH 7 just past Ngahere, turn onto Nelson Creek Road and follow it for 6 km to Nelson Creek. There is an extensive carpark here and picnic area with toilets.

TRACK NOTES

This short walk is particularly good for families with small children as there is a lot to explore in a compact area — a fascinating landscape of tunnels, tailraces and tailings created by gold miners. The tunnels are safe for small children.

From the carpark the track starts, spectacularly, through a short tunnel. Then it crosses the long suspension bridge and around to the start of the Tailrace Walk loop (past the turn-offs to Colls Dam, Callaghans and the Tunnel Walk). The Tailrace Walk is a 20-minute bush circuit, crossing over and around a number of carefully incised tailraces.

Back at the junction with the Tunnel Walk have a look for the start of the tunnel — it can be entered but you will need a torch. There is a small stream and a large swimming hole at the Nelson Creek end.

The suspension bridge that crosses Nelson Creek (23) leads to a swimming hole, trails and short tunnels that are safe for walkers of all ages.

Lastly, return to the signposted Colls Dam Walk and enjoy this peaceful bush circuit past the sleepy Colls Dam and pond. The track continues past the top carpark and crosses numerous deep tailraces.

POINTS OF INTEREST

Nelson Creek was first 'rushed' in 1865 and it has had a long if sporadic history of success and decline. At its height there were 1200 miners working the area, with nine hotels and 30 small businesses; but in practice the gold source proved patchy and unpredictable.

Ground sluicing for gold was the dominant technique used at Nelson Creek, though too much water was as much a nuisance as too little. The miners dug tunnels to gain a healthy pressure of water to scour the gold-bearing gravels and trapped the heavier gold deposits in riffle boxes, but the miners also cut tailraces and sludge channels to drain water and the excess tailings away.

Dredging started from 1900 onwards, once all the easy gold was worked out. Up to 15 gold dredges worked the area, leaving behind the characteristic piles of shingle known as tailings.

24 Croesus Track: Garden Gully Stamping Battery

GRADE 2

TIME Four hours return.

ACCESS From Blackball drive 1 km on Roa Road and turn onto Blackball Road which winds through forest for 4 km to the Smoke-Ho! carpark. The road is narrow and can be rough in places, though most vehicles should manage.

TRACK NOTES

This is a half-day tramp, but a good one. From the Smoke-Ho! carpark the track descends to Smoke-Ho! Creek, which is crossed by a swing bridge. Then the track sidles down to the First Hotel site in a large, grassy clearing.

It is easy walking along the miners' pack track, past Perotti's Mill junction and up to the Second Hotel site, then a couple of lazy zigzags

A berdan, or dish, was used to wash gold ore and is just one of the many remnants of more prosperous days at the Garden Gully Stamping Battery (24).

to the Garden Gully junction. This side-track crosses a saddle down to the old Garden Gully Hut, which has sacking bunks. The track then climbs up a small creek to, arguably, the best-preserved stamping battery on the West Coast.

POINTS OF INTEREST
The Garden Gully mine operated at Dugout Creek from 1905–06, a comparatively short life for all the effort that went into building the massive battery. New huts and a stable block were built during the Depression (the hut that remains dates from this period), but very little gold was extracted.

The Minerva Battery side-tracks have been closed.

25 Croesus Track: Ces Clarke Hut and Croesus Knob

GRADE 3–4
TIME Seven to eight hours return.
ACCESS From Blackball drive 1 km on Roa Road and turn onto Blackball Road which winds through forest for 4 km to the Smoke-Ho! carpark. The road is narrow and can be rough in places, though most vehicles should manage.

TRACK NOTES
This is a longer day's tramp, though not especially difficult as it follows a splendid pack track all the way. It can be done in most weathers but a fine day gives magnificent views from above the Ces Clarke hut.

From the Smoke-Ho! carpark the track descends to Smoke-Ho! Creek, which is crossed by a swing bridge. The track then sidles down to the First Hotel site in a large grassy clearing.

It is easy walking along the miners' pack track, past Perotti's Mill junction and up to the toetoe-fringed Second Hotel site, then a couple of lazy zigzags to the Garden Gully junction. The main Croesus Track continues from Garden Gully in loops upwards, finally breaking out of the bush into a burnt-off area of stumps and flax.

The old Top Hut has three sacking bunks and a fireplace but the hut has been superseded by the Ces Clark Memorial Hut a minute further on. Dedicated to a ranger who died on the track, the hut has a woodstove, sunny verandah and fine views over Grey River/Mawheranui.

The Croesus Track continues and leads into wide tussock basins, sidling underneath and around Croesus Knob. It is worth a brief jaunt up onto

Croesus Knob itself, where there are the remains of the aerial cableway for the Croesus Mine and views of Aoraki/Mt Cook on a fine day.

POINTS OF INTEREST
The Ces Clarke Hut is one of only two mountain huts to be officially opened by a prime minister; in August 1986 David Lange was flown in. The other is the Macauley River Hut in Mackenzie Country, opened by Helen Clarke in 2002.

To be as 'rich as Croesus' is a euphemism for great wealth. Croesus was king of Lydia (560–546 BC) renowned for his wealth. Both Aesop (of fables fame) and Solon (of law-making fame) were drawn to his powerful court.

Gold miners are typically sanguine about the prospects of a gold mine, though from the late 1860s to the 80s the Blackball Creek was very productive indeed. However, much of the early gold was won by sluicing and, later, quartz mining at Garden Gully, Minerva and Croesus Knob proved less profitable.

26 Arnold River Power Station Walk

GRADE 2
TIME One hour for the circuit.
ACCESS This track is well signposted from Stillwater-Moana road. Turn down the access road to the power station, cross the railway line and turn sharp right on the sealed road to the carpark, sign and gate. It is easy to miss the sign.

TRACK NOTES
This is an attractive circuit across the penstock bridge to visit the upper dam, and a return via the bush terrace. There is enough interest for families, and often there are weka scouting about the carpark and picnic areas.

From the carpark, follow the track around the fenceline to the shelter and engraved map. The bridge over the river is actually the pipeline that is carrying the water from the dam. It is not often you walk on a bridge that is mown by a lawnmower! On the other side there is a small picnic area, and from here the track wanders through the bush, and then does a steep zigzag climb to two lookouts towards the Arnold River dam.

The track returns along the bush terrace, often following boardwalks, until it descends in a long zigzag and returns to the bridge by the picnic area.

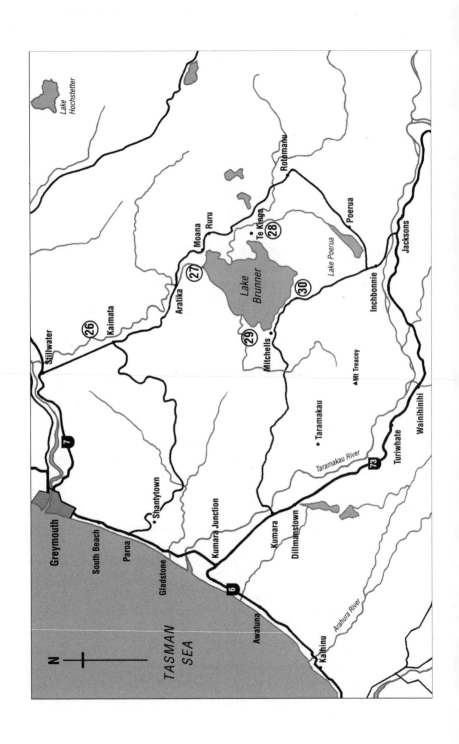

Lake Brunner

Lake Brunner was important to Maori, providing a food source, a transport waterway and an escape from enemies on the pa still called Refuge Island. The lake, known to Maori as Moana, was named after Charles Brunner who was shown the lake by his Maori guides in 1846.

Later, the old Maori trail via Mitchells and Greenstone River was utilised by explorers and gold prospectors. After the gold rush of 1865, farmers gradually moved in and dairy farming and cattle remain important for the region. Moana township and Iveagh Bay are popular with weekenders staying for the boating and fishing on the lake.

Mature forest still surrounds almost 80 percent of the lake's coastline, and many of these short walks wander through the characteristic flax wetlands and kahikatea groves along the lake edge.

27 Rakaitane Walk — Moana

GRADE 1
TIME 30 minutes return.
ACCESS From Moana township take Ahau Street down to the large carpark beside the lake.

The suspension bridge across Arnold River leads to the Rakaitane Walk (27).

TRACK NOTES

The Rakaitane is a great family walk with an impressive swing bridge. From the carpark, follow the track around to the huge swing bridge as it crosses the Arnold River. The water flows barely perceptibly, as it discharges a huge volume of water from Lake Brunner. On the other side of the bridge there is an information sign.

The Rakaitane Walk leads down the river and follows a short loop for 30 minutes. If you travel to the lake instead, the track leads to the soft gravel foreshore where there are various unofficial trails through the lakeside scrub. Or, walk along the foreshore itself.

28 Ara o Te Iringa — Iveagh Bay

GRADE 1–3

TIME Lake and bush circuit, 20 minutes return. Te Iringa bush lookout, three hours return.

ACCESS From the Stillwater-Moana road, the turn-off to Iveagh Bay is 10 km south of Moana. Take the short drive down to the carpark, where there are picnic tables and toilets.

TRACK NOTES

Iveagh Bay is a pleasant and sheltered area, with kahikatea forest growing along the lakeside. Take the main Ara o Te Iringa signposted track and follow the gravelled nature-trail through the forest where there are several tree interpretation signs.

At the four-way junction (not signposted but obvious) head down towards the lake. The gravelled lake shore is quickly reached. The height of the lake varies considerably, but when it is at an average level walkers can stroll along its edge back to the carpark.

The main Te Iringa track continues on a good grade, until it starts to climb and then it becomes a more ordinary trampers' trail. It wanders up a spur beside a creek and reaches the lookout after one hour and 30 minutes. The track to the main summit of Te Kinga is an 8-hour-return walk, with magnificent views of Lake Brunner.

POINTS OF INTEREST

This is a new Te Iringa track, built in 2004 and replacing the old route from Rotomanu railway station.

29 Bains Bay — Mitchells

GRADE 2
TIME Two hours return.
ACCESS Mitchells is found opposite Moana on the other side of Lake Brunner. It can be reached from the Stillwater-Moana road via Lake Poerua, or via Kumara on the road through Greenstone. Parts of the road are unsealed and winding. Directly opposite Lake Brunner Lodge there is an access road down to the lake and a carpark beside the track sign.

TRACK NOTES
This is a beautiful walk, perfect for families as it follows boardwalks through lakeside forest with good views over the lake. Take plenty of sandfly repellent.

From the carpark there are boardwalks that lead past the flax swamps and isolated groves of kahikatea trees around to Carew Bay and a peaceful gravel beach. The track then heads into the forest and climbs a little over a spur around Drake Point and drops to the broad gravel beach of Bains Bay. It is possible to walk along the beach to the Eastern Hohonu river mouth and spit.

POINTS OF INTEREST
The Department of Conservation intends to add more boardwalks to this track, principally to keep the track above lake level. Lake Brunner rises and falls quite rapidly and even the existing boardwalk can become covered.

There has also been the suggestion that the Bains Bay track might eventually be linked with the Rakaitane Walk (27) at Moana in the future.

30 Carew's Creek Waterfall — Mitchells

GRADE 1
TIME 40 minutes return.
ACCESS See above (29) for access to Mitchells. The waterfall is signposted about 100 m before Lake Brunner Lodge.

TRACK NOTES
This is a well-made track to an impressive waterfall. Interesting for children with the bonus that it is all downhill on the return.

This is a steady climb on a well-formed track, through virgin bush and across two short ramps to Carew's Creek and the waterfall.

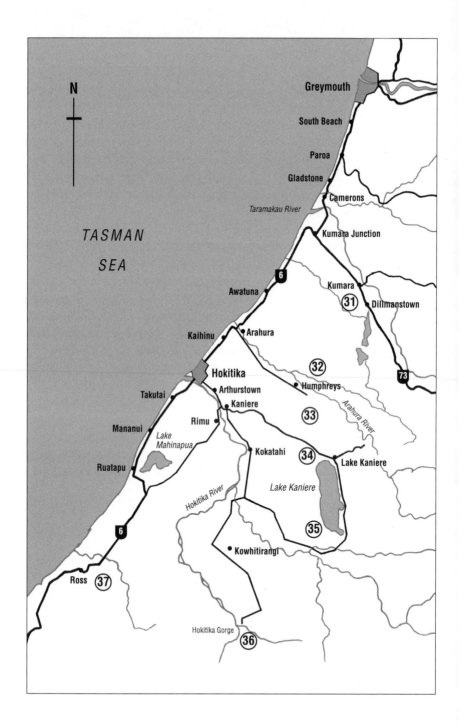

Hokitika and Lake Kaniere

Hokitika was founded by gold miners so it is no surprise that historic gold workings are found everywhere in the Hokitika region, from Kumara to Goldsborough and down to the quiet township of Ross. Tunnels, water races, cemeteries, hand-stacked tailings — all of these features can be explored on the various walks that follow.

Inland from the town of Hokitika is the peaceful haven of Lake Kaniere. There are several elegant walks around this lake, with some exceptional podocarp forest. For something different there is the dramatic chasm of the Hokitika River Gorge.

31 Kumara — Londonderry Rock

GRADE 1

TIME 15 minutes return.

ACCESS Half a kilometre east of Kumara off SH 73 is the hydro-electric access road, and the Londonderry Rock is signposted a short way along here. Follow to a small carpark.

TRACK NOTES

This short walk leads along a well-made path to a huge natural boulder called the 'Londonderry Rock'.

The Kumara gold rush in the 1880s was the last on the West Coast, and all the surrounding land area was cleared of bush and worked for gold. It has since regrown as kanuka and rimu.

The other striking features of this walk are the huge piles of man-made boulder tailings, some of them are easily 5 m high. It was rumoured that when the gold-miners dug underneath Londonderry Rock (to get at the gold underneath), the 'thump' as the rock moved back into the hole could be felt in the Kumara pub.

POINTS OF INTEREST

Several other short family walks can be found around Kumara, including one to the Swimming Baths, signposted just north of Kumara, leading to a large pool still edged by the original stonework (ten minutes). Taylors Hill Walk is a short loop track, signposted off Greenstone Road, that has good views of the Taramakau River and over the town of Kumara (20 minutes).

The start of the Londonderry Rock (31) walk, one of several around Kumara.

32 Goldsborough Track and Roadside Tunnels Track

GRADE 2

TIME One hour 30 minutes to two hours return. This walk describes only a third of the whole Goldsborough Track, which rambles on to the Manzoni Claim at Callaghans Road some 6 km further.

ACCESS From SH 6 turn off at Awatuna onto the Stafford-Dillmanstown road some 10 km to a large carpark, picnic area and campground.

TRACK NOTES

Although a well-graded pack track you will get your feet wet in order to explore these beautiful gold miners' tunnels. The main track initially

A hand-dug gold miners' tunnel, some of which measure up to 30 m long, found on part of the Goldsborough Track (32).

follows Shamrock Creek quite closely through regrowth bush, then crosses the creek beside a bluestone cliff. Over a low spur there is a side-track back down to Shamrock Creek.

There are two tunnels: the first is 100 m downstream, over smooth boulders in the mossy riverbed. It is a wonderful piece of work, and yet this elegant tunnel was only designed to eliminate a bend in the river so as to assist miners in flushing out the tailing debris.

Upstream for five minutes there is an even better tunnel, some 30 m long. Both tunnels are well-fashioned examples of the gold-diggers' art, with crypt-like arched ceilings in the green cloistered riverbed.

POINTS OF INTEREST
The Goldsborough Track continues to Callaghans Road and the Manzoni Claim (grade 2, two hours one way), which has a huge man-made tunnel.

The Roadside Tunnels Track starts 5 km before the Goldsborough carpark off the Stafford-Dillmanstown Road. It is signposted as the Tunnel Terrace Walk beside the small carpark (easy to miss), and children will love it.

It starts through a water-race tunnel, loops around old stone stacks of tailings past the entrances to other tunnels, and emerges on the road through the clever finale of another tunnel. Ten minutes of frolicking fun.

33 Kaniere Water Race

GRADE 2
TIME Three to four hours one way.
ACCESS From Hokitika, take the Lake Kaniere Road some 5 km to the power station carpark and western end of the walkway. Continue to Lake Kaniere to the carpark and picnic area by the control gates. This walk description starts from the Lake Kaniere carpark.
TRACK NOTES
This graceful walkway makes for easy walking, and follows the smooth-flowing water race through bush forest and past tunnels. The first section from Lake Kaniere is good enough for baby buggies.

The first part of the walkway leaves from the control gates by Lake Kaniere and leads through cut-over manuka forest with some emerging kamahi. Freshwater mussels can be seen in the race. It is an easy 3 km to Wards Road and the original Racemans Hut.

The original Racemans Hut, surrounded by a dense forest of rimu and miro, along the Kaniere Water Race (33).

The bush gets thicker and taller in the next section, with ferns underneath the rimu and miro. The race briefly disappears into three tunnels and there are good views of the river below. Tunnel Hill is eventually reached, where a 2 km tunnel takes the water race through to the power station.

The track finally picks up a rather uninteresting bulldozer trail, and descends sharply to a gravel road, which is followed down to the carpark.

POINTS OF INTEREST

The Kaniere Water Race was built in 1875 to provide water to boost the flagging Kaniere goldfield. The water flowed but alas not the gold, so by 1916 the race was utilised for power supply instead and it has remained that way since. The fully automated Kaniere Power Station is one of the smallest in the country and supplies 100–125 houses in Hokitika.

Some parts of the water race still run across flumings — a gold-digger's term for a wooden aqueduct or raised canal. Small leaks in the timber fluming are sealed by the old-fashioned method of throwing sawdust into the water race, which is forced into the cracks. Larger repairs are fixed with new timber that is floated down the race to the repair site.

34 Kahikatea Forest Walk

GRADE 1
TIME 15 minute circuit.
ACCESS From Hokitika, follow the signs to Kaniere and then for about 17 km to Lake Kaniere. At the Sunny Bight foreshore picnic area there are carparks, toilets and signposted walks.
TRACK NOTES
This is a short stroll through an impressive patch of kahikatea forest that follows a pretty stream. Greenery is visible from ground to sky; a dense swathe of ferns at ground level, then mosses and lichens on the trunks of trees and, higher up, epiphytes or perching plants.

The epiphytes are equally diverse: liverworts, mosses, orchids and ferns are present. Plants such as kamahi often begin life as perching seedlings on tree-ferns, and so avoid the gloomy low-life of the forest floor — only one percent of total daylight gets down to the forest floor.

Vines such as supplejack (black), rata (red) and bush lawyer or tataramoa (prickly) survive by climbing quickly towards the light using any convenient tree trunk. Bush lawyer or tataramoa is a close relative of the raspberry and produces very similar looking raspberry-like fruit. The understorey is rich, including kaikomako, mahoe, tree-ferns, coprosmas and many ground ferns. There are over fifty species of fern in the whole Lake Kaniere Scenic Reserve. Prominent birds are the fantail or piwakawaka, grey warbler or riroriro and the bird that parasites its nest, the shining cuckoo or pipiwharauroa — a summer visitor.

POINTS OF INTEREST

Kahikatea is astonishingly productive in terms of its fruit, and this attracts wood pigeons or kereru, bellbirds or korimako, and tui, which in turn help to disperse kahikatea seeds. Kahikatea are New Zealand's tallest native trees, some reaching 60 m in height. Because they like the fertile flood-plain soil, kahikatea were among the first to be cleared when humans needed space for agriculture. The 'white pine' trunks were straight and useful for construction and, because the wood had little 'flavour' to it, it was once used extensively for butter boxes during the country's early exporting days.

Early settlers had a simple nomenclature for the podocarps: kahikatea was 'white pine', rimu 'red pine', matai 'black pine', miro 'brown pine'. The beech forest was often called 'birch' and still portrayed as such on many topographical maps of the 1940s.

35 Lake Kaniere Walkway

GRADE 3

TIME Three to four hours one way.

ACCESS From Hokitika, follow the signs to Kaniere and then for about 17 km to Lake Kaniere. At the Sunny Bight foreshore picnic area there are carparks, toilets and signposted walks.

TRACK NOTES

This half-day walk travels along one side of Lake Kaniere and is suited to strong walkers. Ideally, arrange a pick-up at the end of the walkway, or else leave a vehicle there.

The track is initially well graded and suited to everyone, but after 15 minutes or so a warning sign states that the trail gets rougher and it becomes more of a trampers' track. The forest is lush and there are many picturesque bays with occasional streams running down to the lake shore.

Dorothy Falls can be found a short walk along Lake Kaniere Road, accessible from Lake Kaniere Walkway (35) some 17 km from Hokitika.

Although it touches upon the lake in places, the track mostly stays above and meanders onto the beach and old hut called Lawyers Delight. This hut is still useable. There is then a short climb around the side of Mt Upright and through cut-over forest to the carpark beside Lake Kaniere Road.

POINTS OF INTEREST

Lake Kaniere is unusual because it is almost completely surrounded by forest, a great habitat for bush birds including bellbird or korimako, yellow breasted tomtit or miromiro, brown creeper and the tiny rifleman, New Zealand's smallest bird. The Maori named this bird titipounamu, which could be translated to signify a small piece of greenstone.

Another very short walk beside the Lake Kaniere Road and carpark is to the splendid Dorothy Falls.

36 Hokitika Gorge

GRADE 1

TIME 15 minutes return.

ACCESS From Hokitika, follow the signs to Kaniere, then the signposts to Kokatahi, Kowhitirangi and on to the Hokitika Gorge carpark.

TRACK NOTES

This is a short walk down to a highly scenic gorge. Follow the track through the podocarp forest down to the long swing bridge over the Hokitika River.

Stunningly coloured blue-green water, resembling liquid greenstone or pounamu, passes slowly under the bridge. The track continues over the bridge, and scrambles around to the top end (upstream) of the gorge.

POINTS OF INTEREST

There is currently a commercial proposal to construct a rainforest canopy walk beside the gorge.

37 Ross Goldfields Water Race Walk

GRADE 2

TIME One hour for the circuit.

ACCESS Ross is 30 km south of Hokitika, and this walk starts from the Ross Visitor Centre, carpark and toilets. There is also a historic prison cell to visit (with inmate).

The track through the old Ross cemetery can be found along the Water Race Walk (37).

TRACK NOTES

This is a good walk for children, especially if you start at the top carpark. From the Visitor Centre, walk up Mt Greenland Road. After a kilometre this leafy and narrow lane reaches a carpark and a signpost stating that only 4WD vehicles can go further. The Water Race walkway starts here.

The track is easy-walking past old gold workings, several tunnel entrances, a reconstructed fluming and, later, a reconstructed miner's hut. Once out of the bush there is a view of Ross township.

The track winds through the lovely and historic cemetery to St James Street and returns to the Ross Visitor Centre.

POINTS OF INTEREST

On 10 September 1909, the largest gold nugget ever found in New Zealand was discovered by John Scott and Arthur Sharp at Ross. The nugget was the size of a man's hand and weighed 99 ounces (3.1 kg); it was dubbed the 'Honourable Roddy'. It was later bought by the government and presented to King George V where it was turned into a golden tea service for Buckingham Palace.

The Jones Flat Walk in this area was located on private land but was eroded by the functioning of the open-cast goldmine. This goldmine has now ceased operation and the large hole is filling with water. Once stabilised, this attractive arena will be turned into a recreational lake and reserve.

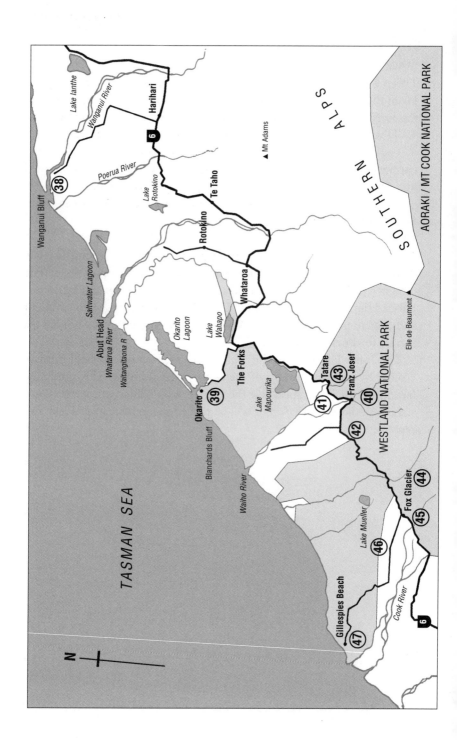

Lagoons and Glaciers

South of Hokitika and Ross, the West Coast scenery becomes grand, with a series of inland lakes, great glaciers and the twin peaks of Aoraki/Mt Cook and Mt Tasman looming over coastal lagoons. Dense forest laps along the main highway itself and settlements seem few and far between.

Many of the best walks are clustered around the two glacier towns of Franz and Fox, but don't forget the remote Harihari Coastal Walkway (38) inland from Harihari, or the charming old gold miners' pack tracks on the Okarito (39).

Along with the large dollops of scenery come large dollops of sandflies and buckets of rain, so an insect repellent and a good raincoat are essential. It can often be raining at the glaciers, yet rain-free on the coast at Gillespies Beach (47) or Okarito lagoon. The sunsets at both those beaches are marvellous.

38 Harihari Coastal Walkway

GRADE 2

TIME Two hours 30 minutes to three hours for the circuit.

ACCESS From Harihari on SH 6 turn down Wanganui Flat Road (the walkway is signposted) and drive to the coast some 20 km to the small carpark. Note: it is much easier to have a mid to low tide for the round trip.

TRACK NOTES

This is an interesting circuit track to a coastal headland and lookout platform, where all there is to see is pristine wilderness. There is a splendid beach and headland, several quirky whitebaiters' baches and some comfortable stretches along a historic pack track, making it a good walk for older children.

From the carpark, the coastal walkway passes the return junction and then ambles alongside the Wanganui River past several whitebaiters' stands and huts. The track skirts kahikatea forest and swampland before crossing tidal mud flats to the base of Mt One One.

The view of pristine wilderness from the lookout at Mt One One, on Harihari Coastal Walkway (38).

Steps lead up to the excellent viewing platform, and you might notice on the way up the numerous burrows underneath the stairway, home to a shearwater colony. From Mt One One, drop back to the junction and stroll along this driftwood-strewn beach. At low tide it is easy to get around the point, and wander past some large sculptured rocks. There is also an alternative high-tide bush track.

The Poerua River is not as large as the Wanganui and, in winter, river levels can get so low that the sea builds up a permanent gravel bar across the mouth. The track skirts the river through sand and tidal flats to several whitebaiters' shanties. The track then turns inland and follows the well-laid line of the old pack track, crossing a low 100-m saddle, and drops to the Pakihi Swamp on the other side and the carpark.

POINTS OF INTEREST
Mt One One is a distinctive moraine hillock at the mouth of the Wanganui River. In 1865, Charlie Douglas commented, 'It had the honour of being the first scene in Westland that appeared in the *Illustrated London News*. Home people must have had some fun over the name, so suggestive of the first numeral, and wondered at Colonial nomenclature, never dreaming the name One One is Maori.' The meaning of the name is still obscure, though 'Oue' is suggested as an alternative name.

The sooty shearwater or titi are the most well-known of the shearwaters that are eaten as 'muttonbirds', a delicacy among Maori. Generally black-brown in appearance, the shearwaters come back to their burrows around October, tidying them up in preparation for mating. Eggs are laid from November to December, the hatchlings are out by January and the young ready to leave the burrow by April or May. Shearwaters migrate to the northern hemisphere during the New Zealand winter.

39 Okarito Pack Track

GRADE 2–3
TIME Three to four hours return. One hour return to Okarito trig.
ACCESS From The Forks turn-off, 16 km south of Whataroa on SH 6, it is a 13-km trip along a sealed road to Okarito. There is a camping ground, information post (in the wharf shed), signposted walks and boat launching ramp. Tide tables are found at the beach noticeboard.
TRACK NOTES
This is one of the best walking circuits on the West Coast. A historic bush

pack track in one direction, and an easy beach walk the other with a short side-trip up to Okarito trig and lookout. A low to mid tide is essential for the beach section.

From the roadside sign found just before the beach carpark, the pack track climbs up to a track junction with the Okarito trig. If the day is fine this is a most worthwhile side-trip up to a lookout platform, with views of Okarito in the foreground and the long horizon filled with the snowy peaks of the Southern Alps.

The main pack track rolls along to Three Mile Lagoon, coming close to the cliff edge at times, with a good crop of ferns and mosses beside the track. It drops sharply to a junction; the left-hand fork leads to a long bridge over the Three Mile Lagoon; the right-hand fork to a wide beach. The lagoon entrance is often blocked by a sand and gravel bar.

Walkers can also venture along the beach to the next lagoon named the Five Mile or Totaranui, which during the gold rush of July 1866 boasted five hotels, 40 stores, two butcher shops and two bakeries, with a population of 1500. But the gold-rich black sands were quickly exhausted and by December that year the population plummeted to 300.

Three Mile Lagoon along the Okarito Pack Track (39), with Mt Tasman and Aoraki/Mt Cook in the distance.

From Three Mile lagoon, the beach walk back to Okarito at low tide is easy and exhilarating with the restless surf rolling in. There is not much rock-hopping needed and a seal occasionally hauls ashore.

POINTS OF INTEREST
Packhorses were utilised to get around Kohuamarua Bluff or Te Kohuamaru, ironically described by Gerhard Mueller as 'this fine piece of Queen's Highway':

'It used to be a study watching a long line of loaded packhorses with perhaps only one man driving. Going round a bluff in heavy weather, the loads were usually from 250 to 300 lbs of very mixed character. The horses that were up to the work could watch the seas far better than most men. A good packer never swore, or threw stones at his horse, but let them take their own time, the animals would all stop and watch as sea coming in, then make a run for it. If by chance they got caught, they had a way of propping themselves face or back to the waves, and holding their own, then as the sea receded off they went at a trot.'

Maori legend has it that the white heron or kotuku is so rare that it is seen only once in a lifetime. In fact, their winter dispersal takes them to estuaries all over New Zealand including the Avon-Heathcote estuary in the heart of Christchurch city, but they breed only at Waitangiroto, a river just north of Okarito lagoon. The nests are perched high up in the kahikatea and often shared with spoonbills and little shags or kawau.

40 Franz Josef Glacier/Ka Roimata o Hine Walk

GRADE 2
TIME One to two hours return.
ACCESS From Franz Josef/Waiau village on SH 6 it is 5 km to the glacier carpark, information signs and toilets. Some 4 km of this road is gravelled, and the narrow road can at times get busy.
TRACK NOTES
This is a flat walk over river gravel to the snout of the Franz Josef Glacier/ Ka Roimata o Hine. Great views can be had of the surrounding mountains and their steep carved walls.

Follow the well-marked track out onto the Waiho riverbed, as the trail snakes among river boulders. Here there are many good views of the waterfalls that pour down the steep rock faces.

The actual glacier snout is roped off and walkers are advised not to go

The start of the one hour journey up the riverbed to Franz Josef Glacier/Ka Roimata o Hine (40).

beyond the roped-off area unless they are part of a guided glacier tour. Blocks of ice fall from the face regularly, hence the precautions.

Sometimes in the short term the glacier edges forwards, usually five to six years after heavy snowfalls in the neve, but the long-term outlook for this particular glacier (like most of the other glaciers around the world) is a steady and slow retrenchment.

POINTS OF INTEREST

The Maori name for Franz Josef Glacier — Ka Roimata o Hine(-hukatere) — translates as 'the tears of Hinehukatere'. Fox Glacier is also called Te Moeka o Tuawe, or 'the bed of Tuawe' in Maori.

Franz Josef was originally known as Waiho or Waiho Gorge, a corruption of Waiau, a common Maori name meaning 'swirling waters'.

An English couple named Batson arrived in the 1890s and built a ponga house which became known as Batson's 'hotel', the first accommodation at Franz Josef/Waiau. Maud Moreland stayed in the hotel in 1906 and remarked that 'a house of this kind may even grow, for the ferns are very tenacious of life'.

41 Franz Josef Glacier/Ka Roimata o Hine: short walks

GRADE 1–2
TIME Varies.
ACCESS All day walks begin from Franz Josef/Waiau township.
TRACK NOTES
There are several short bush walks around the Franz Josef/Waiau village area. The Terrace Walk starts almost opposite the DoC Visitor Centre and ambles through bush to an old gold miners' water race and tailings, with a view of the Waiho River (25 minutes return).

The Tartare Tunnel Walk starts behind Franz Josef/Waiau village at the signposted carpark and leads up a wide gravel road to the junction with Callery Gorge-Waiho River track. The road continues down to Tartare River, then a short track zigzags up to the old Tartare water tunnel. This can be explored for a short distance, but take a torch and be prepared to get your feet wet (one hour 30 minutes return).

The Callery Gorge-Waiho Track sidles from the Tartare Tunnel junction through bush and crosses the swing bridge over the dramatic Callery Gorge. The track then sidles along the Waiho River to the historic Douglas swing bridge. Some walkers use this track as a means of walking to the

Franz Josef Glacier/Ka Roimata o Hine (two hours one way to the bridge, and four hours one way to the glacier).

Canavans Knob Track is a pleasant out-of-town sojourn to the top of a bush-covered granite outcrop. The carpark is found on top of a stopbank. The track winds up gently from here through rata forest to a seat and lookout towards the glacier (30 minutes return).

Another popular short walk is to Sentinel Rock, a roche moutonne or large glacial rock that was once covered by the glacier. There are excellent information panels here and a good scramble for smaller children (15 minutes return).

The Douglas Walk and Peters Pool Walk can be connected in a one-hour-return circuit. The track is signposted off the glacier road (small carpark on the Lake Wombat side), and wanders through bush to the historic swing bridge over the Waiho River. It then continues along to Peters Pool, a peaceful kettle lake. This can be a perfect spot for reflection photos. Return along the road, which is narrow and can be busy.

42 Franz Josef Glacier/Ka Roimata o Hine: Lake Wombat and Alex Knob

GRADE 4

TIME Seven to eight hours return (a full day tramp).

ACCESS From SH 6, take the Glacier Access Road some 3 km to Douglas Bridge carpark.

TRACK NOTES

A steep and steady pack track, originally built as a tourist trail, leads to the summit of Alex Knob. This offers a magnificent viewpoint, though the walk is only worth attempting on a fine day. It is more properly a trampers' track than a walkers' track.

From the carpark, the track climbs gradually to Lake Wombat, a kettle lake surrounded by forest (one hour 15 minutes return). From here the pack track climbs steadily, and there are not many views up the bush ridge until the tussock tops are reached. There are magnificent views here, but park rangers advise an early start on this track before the afternoon cloud rolls over and obscures the view of the mountains. Alex Knob is 1303 m above sea level.

POINTS OF INTEREST

Like all the West Coast coastal ranges Alex Knob receives an enormous amount of rain. During March 1982, the rain gauge recorded 181 cm in just three days.

43 Franz Josef Glacier/Ka Roimata o Hine: Point Roberts Track

GRADE 3–4

TIME Five to six hours return.

ACCESS From SH 6, take the Glacier Access Road some 3 km to Douglas Bridge carpark.

TRACK NOTES

This is an adventurous up-and-down bush track with a scramble up a ladder, over three suspension bridges and a boardwalk bolted into the rock.

From the carpark cross the flat bush to the historic Douglas Bridge, then across Hugh Creek as the track winds up and down, with a staircase at one point, through dense rata and kamahi forest before climbing abruptly to a swing bridge across Arch Creek.

The track sidles across bare schist rock and scrubby slopes to a well-situated seat and the old Hendes Hut shelter. From here there is a steep

The view from Point Roberts (43) is a reward for the adventurous day walker.

descent along the boardwalk that is bolted into the rock-face. Then the track climbs again and crosses the dramatically incised Rope Creek on a swaying swing bridge.

It is a steady climb over slippery rocks, then a long sidle before Point Roberts is reached. The scenery becomes absorbing as the tremendous scale of the Franz Josef Glacier/Ka Roimata o Hine icefall becomes clear.

POINTS OF INTEREST
Hendes Hut was named after Peter Hende who supervised the building of this track in 1906. Point Roberts was the tourist route to the glacier up to the 1930s, before the glacier's recession made it redundant.

44 Fox Glacier/Te Moeka o Tuawe Walk

GRADE 2
TIME One hour return.
ACCESS Off SH 6 by the Fox River, follow the signposted glacier road to the carpark. Due to river floods this road is often subject to change and closure, but the drive in across the Fox River flood plain and under the cliffs of Cone Rock is magnificent. Kea frequent the carpark.

TRACK NOTES
A short impressive walk over old moraines to the foot of the Fox Glacier. From the carpark the track climbs over some large humps, which are actually lumps of old glacier ice covered in rock. Views are good already as the trail winds over the scree slope, and crosses the stream over a footbridge.

You cannot touch the ice, for obvious reasons, and the glacier tongue is roped off. But you can feel the icy air rolling off the glacier, and photograph an object that, if you came back next month will have moved on.

POINTS OF INTEREST
'Weheka' was an early name for Fox Glacier. The nearby township was virtually 'invented' by one man — Mick Sullivan. He swapped a parcel of land owned by the family with a small area of 11 acres from the Crown. 'When the Commissioner asked why Mick wanted the 11 acres the reply was: 'If we are to stay in this region we need a village.' The land was divided into freehold sections which became Fox village.

45 Fox Glacier/Te Moeka o Tuwae: short walks

GRADE 1–2

TIME Varies.

ACCESS All from Fox township.

TRACK NOTES

There are several short forest walks around the Fox Glacier/Te Moeka o Tuwae area, and all are signposted. The Minehaha Walk starts just south of the township and is a well-graded track that follows a pretty stream (20 minutes one way).

The Ngai Tahu Track, named for the dominant Maori tribe of the South Island, is a longer climb through bush terraces to a peat swamp. This circuit begins from the Minehaha Walk (one hour 30 minutes).

From Glacier View Road on the south bank of the Fox River, there is the short Moraine Walk (20 minutes) as well as the River Walk (15 minutes), both of which cross a historic swing bridge to Glacier View Road.

The Chalet Lookout Track begins from the end of Glacier View Road and leads to a bush lookout with views of Fox Glacier/Te Moeka o Tuwae (Grade 3, one hour 30 minutes to two hours return). This track winds

This swing bridge crosses the Fox River and leads to the Moraine and River walks, just two of many short walks around Fox Glacier/Te Moeka o Tuwae (45).

through attractive rata and kamahi forest, with red rata flowers in the summer months. Two streams are crossed and the Fluted Falls are passed. After a short climb, walkers have to scramble across Boulder Creek and, later, the much larger Mills Creek which can cause problems after rain. It is a few minutes further to the lookout.

Last century, Fox Glacier/Te Moeka o Tuwae terminal icefall was directly below the Chalet lunch hut, and glacier walkers could view the ice while eating lunch on the balcony. However, the glacier has since dramatically retreated and the lunch hut has gone, leaving just the track behind.

46 Lake Matheson

GRADE 2

TIME One hour 30 minutes to two hours return.

ACCESS From Fox Glacier/Te Moeka o Tuwae village drive 5 km to the signposted carpark. Toilets and a café are here.

TRACK NOTES

Lake Matheson is a popular walking and photographing spot, particularly with people trying to photograph the famous 'view of views': Aoraki/Mt Cook and Tasman reflected in the lake. Most people travel clockwise around the lake, and it is a good walk for family groups.

The track first crosses the Clearwater Stream bridge and leads to the first viewpoint, but walkers must venture further to the head of the lake and climb up to the View of Views platform to get the classic view seen on many tablemats and calendars. On the way, the rich rainforest is made of tall kahikatea, rimu and matai with a lush understorey of shrubs and ferns. Look out for perching orchids on logs and stumps.

A few minutes on from the View of Views, there is a side-track to Reflection Island, a particularly pretty perch beside the lake. The famous reflections result partly from the brown colouration of the water, which is caused by organic matter leached from the humus on the forest floor. The calm surface of the lake accentuates any bird sound.

The main track then moves away from the lake and follows the forest around to farm paddocks with splendidly isolated kahikatea trees.

POINTS OF INTEREST

Lake Matheson was formed from a large chunk of ice that got left behind when the Fox Glacier/Te Moeka o Tuwae ice sheet retreated about 14,000 years ago, leaving mounds of moraine debris that trapped the resultant lake — technically called a 'kettle lake'.

The bushbirds most likely heard are the bellbird or korimako, yellow breasted tomtit or miromiro and fantail or piwakawaka, as well as the cheerful song thrush and the alarming squawks of blackbirds. On the water, paradise shelducks or putangitangi honk in lugubrious pairs, and mallards fossick in the reedy edges.

A trampers' track, which is usually muddy, is marked from Lake Matheson to Lake Gault (one hour one way).

47 Gillespies Beach and seal colony

GRADE 2

TIME Two hours return to the lagoon. Three hours to the historic tunnel and lookout. Four hours return to the seal colony.

ACCESS From Fox Glacier/Te Moeka o Tuwae township it is 20 km to Gillespies Beach, and 11 km of this is an unsealed, narrow and difficult road with many blind corners. Watch out for campervans. Gillespies Beach has a carpark, toilets and signposted walks.

TRACK NOTES

This is an interesting coastal walk that visits a lagoon estuary, a seal colony, and follows a historic pack track through a tunnel. There is plenty to keep children interested on this walk.

From the carpark, follow the track through the sand dunes and gorse to where the old gold dredge ruins are slowly mouldering into the mire. Cross to the beach and travel north to the lagoon estuary.

A long trestle bridge crosses the dark tidal waters and leads onto a well-made pack track that was once the main road along the West Coast, before the inland bridleways were made. The pack track leads through swamp and coastal forest and climbs to a junction; the left branch takes you to the tunnel and lookout.

The tunnel was cut in the 1890s to avoid the awkward Gillespies Point headland. From here, descend to the beach and it takes 30 minutes north to Galway Beach and the fur seal colony. It is mainly a resting colony during the non-breeding winter season, with up to 1500 seals present. During the summer this declines to about 30–40 immature bull seals. Do not disturb the seals, and if intending to go further north, take the alternative inland track. The inland track from the tunnel to

The trestle bridge that spans this tranquil lagoon leads to a pack track through a variety of forest vegetation to a lookout and tunnel. The track then descends to Gillespies Beach and the fur seal colony (47).

Galway Beach is usually very muddy and more of a tramping track than a walking track.

The lookout from the trig is impressive, particularly if the nearby rata is flowering.

POINTS OF INTEREST

James Edwin Gillespie found gold here in 1865 and Gillespies Beach soon 'rushed' to 700 miners, three hotels, two bakeries and two butchers.

The gold-rich black sands led to extraordinary rushes at many South Westland beaches in the 1860s, most notably at Three Mile and Five Mile (both just south of Okarito). Towns literally sprang up overnight as the miners jostled, fought and swore to be the first to 'peg out' a claim. Some claims were spectacularly rich, diggers washing several ounces of gold after a couple of hours' work. However, black sand claims were quickly worked out — sometimes even in hours — and once the first rush of miners had exhausted the obvious gold leads there would always be a few 'hatters' left: solitary miners making a bare living.

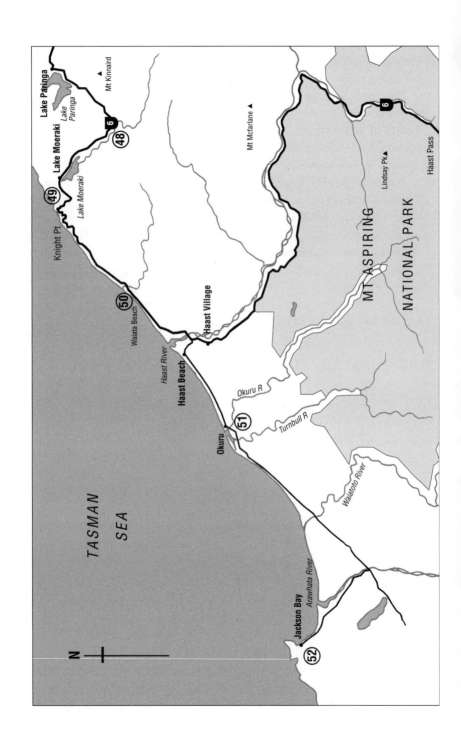

South Westland and Haast

South Westland, even by West Coast standards, is remote and isolated. Haast was finally connected with a through-road only as late as 1965, and since then has become part of a tourist scenic loop, connecting the West Coast with Wanaka and Otago.

The scenery is unstinting down here, with forest running from the wild shoreline right up to the high mountains. This is one of the last untamed areas of New Zealand and there is little human encroachment beyond the roadside.

There are many fine short walks in this region — some that explore to the rugged beaches, such as Monro Beach (49), Ship Creek (50), and others explore into estuaries like the Hapuka River (51). Two excellent longer walks are up the Paringa Cattle Track (48) or to the remote Smoothwater Bay (52).

48 Paringa Cattle Track

GRADE 3–4

TIME Two to three hours return to Blowfly Hut. Six to seven hours return to Maori Saddle Hut.

ACCESS From SH 6, signposted 5 km south of Lake Moeraki.

TRACK NOTES

This is a historic cattle road on a good benched track, though it can be wet and muddy underfoot. It is a long daytrip to Maori Saddle and back, so start early.

From the carpark, the track is muddy at first, then it joins the original cattle trail and sidles through bush over to the big suspension bridge over Moeraki (or Blue) River. Blowfly Hut, an old roadman's hut, sits in a clearing.

From here the excellently graded track begins its slow journey up to Maori Saddle Hut. The forest is rich in rimu and silver beech and the bird life is equally profuse. Kereru, tomtits or miromiro, fantails or piwakawaka, bellbirds or korimako, and kaka add sound to a rarely

Blowfly Hut sits in a clearing on the Paringa Cattle Track (48). The more spacious Maori Saddle Hut is found an hour along the track.

silent forest. Old totara posts on the trackside indicate the telegraph line, and the flat stones in the creeks were laid to make the passage of the cattle easier.

After an hour the narrow Whakapohai Saddle is reached, and a short time later there is a side-track up to a mica mine. The main track climbs steadily and meanders past several side-creeks (Thompson, Stormy and finally the Whakapohai itself), then descends to the spacious hut at Maori Saddle. This hut stands in a cleared beech glade, has 12 bunks and a woodstove. It is a cosy place to stop for lunch, especially as rain is not unheard of in this locality, and there is a long, easy romp downhill to look forward to.

POINTS OF INTEREST

The Haast-Paringa Cattle Track was built in 1871 following the line of a Maori trail, and then developed as a pack track for diggers. It was designed to avoid the awkward stretch of coastline around Knights Point and climbs over a 609 m saddle.

Cattle were taken in mobs of 200 from the South Westland river valleys like the Arawata and Cascade, mustered along the beach to the Waita River and brought to graze near Copper Creek Hut. In the pre-dawn, cattle were then broken into smaller mobs to prevent them bunching on narrow parts of the track, and pushed over the saddle to be corralled at the Moeraki River, near Blowfly Hut.

49 Monro Beach

GRADE 2

TIME Two hours return.

ACCESS Follow SH 6 to Lake Moeraki Lodge and take the short signposted side-road to the carpark and information signs.

TRACK NOTES

A beautiful walk, good for families, which plunges the visitor into a thick forest of mixed podocarp and kiekie vine to a sheltered and attractive bay.

From the carpark, the trail follows a vehicle track and crosses a footbridge over Monro Creek. A short distance further the Monro Track leaves the vehicle track and heads into the forest. It then crosses a low saddle and drops gently to the sandy bay.

A colony of Fiordland crested penguins nests in the forest behind the northern part of Munro Beach, and visitors are asked not to pass beyond the penguin sign if birds are seen on the beach.

POINTS OF INTEREST

The Fiordland crested penguin is one of the world's rarest birds, and they are strikingly attractive with red beaks and a prominent yellow flash above the eye which ends in a noticeable tuft of feathers. The penguins will climb well up thick bush slopes to find a suitable nesting spot — under a fallen log for example — and return to the same place year after year. They lay a clutch of two eggs in August–September, the young birds are fledged by November–December and ready for an independent life.

Kiekie is a thick coastal vine and a relative of the tropical pandanus, which manages to live in these southern frost-free coastal situations. It attaches itself to a holding tree and sends out a mass of aerial roots, forming large tangled clumps at ground level. Kiekie can grow profusely on coastal spurs and is rarely found far inland. Maori still use the leaves for weaving, and the pulp of the ripe fruit was also eaten once the bitter-tasting skin was removed.

50 Ship Creek — Dune Walk and Swamp Walk

GRADE 1

TIME One hour return for both walks.

ACCESS Ship Creek is signposted 10 km north of Haast on SH 6, and has a carpark, toilets, an information sign and large shelter with a tower.

TRACK NOTES

These are two beautiful and short walks, one illustrating the dune and coastal environment while the other leads around a bush wetland. Both walks are superb, and suitable for young and older children. Take plenty of sandfly repellent.

The Dune Walk begins underneath the lookout tower and information signs, and follows an elongated loop through dunes topped by the orange-red native pingao. The walk wanders through coastal forest to reach a beautiful inland lagoon before turning back to the carpark.

The Swamp Walk starts from the tower, and dives under the roadbridge alongside the dark and slow-moving Ship Creek. It reaches a junction then circles through wetland forest. Sometimes, if there has been a lot of rain, the track itself is flooded, but usually the boardwalk rises just above this wetland.

Idyllic morning at Ship Creek (50), one of the few day walks that explores both dune and coastal environments.

There is a magnificent kahikatea tree halfway along the Swamp Walk with an information panel describing how bountiful such a tree is for bird life.

POINTS OF INTEREST

The Maori name for Ship Creek is Tauparikaka.

The ship that gave the creek its name was once part of the *Schomberg*; 26,000 tons and constructed of wood, it was grounded on a sandbank at Cape Otway, Australia in 1855 on its maiden voyage. The ship disintegrated and part of it drifted to the West Coast — there is no evidence of it now.

51 Hapuka Estuary

GRADE 1

TIME 30 minutes for the circuit.

ACCESS From Haast drive 15 km to Okuru to the Haast Motor Camp. The walk is signposted 50 m down a side road, where there is a carpark.

TRACK NOTES

This is a short, attractive loop track with good views of Open Bay Islands. Children will enjoy this little circuit.

The track starts in the coastal kowhai forest, which grows on the work of other plants like native broom or taineka, tutu, and flax or harakeke, which have fixed nitrogen from the air into the black river silts. Under the kowhai there are understorey plants such as manuka.

Birds from normally different cultures mix together here; bush birds like bellbird or korimako, wood pigeon or kereru, tui, yellow-breasted tomtit or miromiro, grey warbler or riroriro and fantail or piwakawaka can be seen almost side by side with estuary-lovers such as bittern or matuka, pukeko, oystercatcher or torea and pied stilt or poaka. In the waters there are flounder or patiki, eel or tuna, common bully and yellow-eyed mullet or aua, as well as mud crabs and mudflat snails or titiko.

An information panel explains the whitebait story, then the track leaves the estuary and wanders into a rich rimu forest with kiekie vine tangled through it. There is an excellent lookout towards the two Open Bay Islands in the Tasman Sea.

POINTS OF INTEREST

Whitebait are the young of five varieties of a native fish species called galaxiids, of which the most prolific is the inanga. In autumn, the female inanga lays eggs in the lower rivers and estuaries and the male releases milt

The superb view over Hapuka Estuary (51), home to an abundance of marine and bird life.

to fertilise them. This milt can cloud the creeks. Most adult inanga then die, while the eggs hatch into larvae and catch the big tides out to sea. In spring the young fish (or whitebait) migrate back up the river, which is where the whitebaiters are waiting …

The Open Bay Islands, which can be seen from the lookout, are called Taumaka and Popotai and were used as a source of muttonbird and seabird eggs by Maori. They are still retained in Maori ownership. The bay was originally named by Captain Cook as 'Open Bay', but was changed to Jackson Bay/Okahu and the name fell onto these two small islands.

A sealing party landed on Open Bay Islands in 1810 from the *Active*, and they gathered some 11,000 seal skins but their ship was lost at sea, marooning them for almost four years. The party survived on seal meat and a 'species of fern'. They were rescued when John Grono, on the brig *Governor Bligh*, arrived coincidentally. John Grono was the first European to sight Milford Sound, initially naming it Milford Haven.

The word kowhai is the colour yellow in Maori and is the national flower of New Zealand. It is a showy tree in spring and can be found almost anywhere in the country. Kowhai seeds are hard and can float, staying viable over long distances — which might explain why there is also a species found in Chile, as well as eight species here. In the wild, kowhai is pollinated by the bellbird or korimako, and tui, but it grows easily in the garden. The wood is durable and elastic and has been used for axe handles and other garden tools.

52 Jackson Bay/Okahu — Smoothwater Bay

GRADE 3

TIME Three to four hours return.

ACCESS From Haast, at SH 6, follow the sealed road some 45 km to Jackson Bay/Okahu, and the information shelter and toilets.

TRACK NOTES
The track to Smoothwater Bay starts just before the shelter. Wet feet are unavoidable — it's part of the fun.

The marked track begins at Jackson Bay/Okahu, following the old pack track that was probably travelled by Polish settlers in 1875. A gentle climb over a saddle is easily managed, before slipping down to Smoothwater River. This river is a wide shining path, rarely more than knee-deep and on soft, easy gravels. On a sunny day, splashing down the river is delightful. The thick bush is full of bird song and it is approximately 1.5 km to the coast, crossing the river on average eight to ten times.

The beach is a curvaceous curl of sand, and at low tide it is possible to explore along either shoreline. At Smoothwater Bay there is a grass terrace overlooking the attractive bay.

POINTS OF INTEREST
The Wharekai Te Kau Walk starts from Jackson Bay/Okahu and leads over a low bush saddle to the rocky shoreline (30 minutes return).

In the 1870s, Jackson Bay/Okahu was the scene of an ill-fated government settlement. The early colonists at the settlement were a mixed bag of Irish, English, Polish (who chose to go to Smoothwater Bay), Scottish, German, Scandinavian (mostly at Waiatoto) and Italian (mainly at Okuru). Some settlers were clearly out of their depth; Pietro Tofanari, a former hotel waiter, wrote '… the beginning I find very bad in this bushy bushy country'. By 1885, apart from a few families that stayed, the settlement was finished. It cost the government about £30,000.

Maori have lived in the vicinity of Jackson Bay/Okahu for centuries, and in the 1850s one account suggests up to 200–300 people in a village at Arawhata or Okuru. The area was probably a major base for the manufacture of greenstone or pounamu tools and ornaments.

It is likely that sealers and whalers used Jackson Bay/Okahu, perhaps for out of season work, taking advantage of the good harbour and timber to do repairs on their boats and buying vegetables from Maori.